August 7th 1988

Debra Shipley and M̲_____s
working in both bro_____s.
Their interests are wide and varied, ranging from parks to
pageantry, culture to crafts, drawing to jogging.

Happy Birthday Dad

Love Sue & Alistair

By the same authors

DEBRA SHIPLEY
and MARY PEPLOW

Glasgow for Free

GRAFTON BOOKS

A Division of the Collins Publishing Group

LONDON GLASGOW
TORONTO SYDNEY AUCKLAND

Grafton Books
A Division of the Collins Publishing Group
8 Grafton Street, London W1X 3LA

A Grafton Paperback Original 1988

Copyright © Debra Shipley and Mary Peplow 1988

ISBN 0-586-07316-7

Printed and bound in Great Britain by
Collins, Glasgow

Set in Times

Contents

Acknowledgements

Throughout our research, particularly during our stay in Glasgow, we consistently received help, hospitality and encouragement. We couldn't possibly name all the people who provided us with information, offered support, and pointed us in the right direction to discover the hidden facets of Glasgow. However, we would like to say a special thank you to some of the individuals: Patricia and Tom Douglas, John Fox, Alice Mackensie, Joyce Mac-Lennan, Sarah Salway and Frank Arneil Walker (author of *Clyde Estuary South*, an architectural guide to Inverclyde and Renfrew Districts, published by RIAS and Scottish Academic Press, 1986).

We're also enormously grateful for the help we received from British Caledonian Airways for transporting us swiftly from our base in London; and to Stakis Hotels and Inns Ltd for providing us with a comfortable 'home' at the Ingram Hotel right in the heart of Glasgow. And, of course, thanks to the Greater Glasgow Tourist Board and Glasgow District Council for their keen support of our project.

Preface

We've thoroughly enjoyed exploring Greater Glasgow, and we've been especially delighted by the sheer quality of the things to see and do for free in and around the city. Some entries in the book, such as the Burrell Collection, deservedly have an international reputation; others, such as the Barony Chambers Museum, might be smaller and little known but are of an impressively high standard.

We hope that *Glasgow for Free* will help you make the most of Greater Glasgow. The information has been organized under chapter headings and each entry has an address and, when available, a telephone number. If appropriate, opening times have been supplied. At the time of going to press all practical details were correct. Although the book is full of things of interest, we're sure there's plenty more to discover in Greater Glasgow, so if you feel there's something else that deserves a mention, do write and tell us about it.

For further information contact: the Greater Glasgow Tourist Board, 35–39 St Vincent Place, Glasgow G1 2ER. Tel: 041-227 4885.
For travel information contact: Strathclyde Transport Information Centre, St Enoch Square, Glasgow G1. Tel: 041-226 4826 (open all year, Monday–Saturday 0930–1730; June–September, Sunday 1200–1400. Telephone hours: all year, Monday–Saturday 0700–midnight, Sunday 0900–2100).

Message from The Rt Hon The Lord Provost Robert Gray OStJ JP

'Glasgow's miles better' is our slogan, and with a copy of this imaginative and informative book, *Glasgow for Free*, citizens and visitors alike are sure to find that our boast is not without good cause.

Discovering the diversities of Glasgow will be an exciting and interesting process. In addition, there is the promise of a few surprises when you discover how much you can do for free.

Much meticulous research has gone into the production of this book, and it can only be of tremendous value and benefit to those who read it, and indeed to the city itself.

Robert Gray

Glasgow's Coat of Arms

Glasgow's Coat of Arms was granted to the city in 1866. The half-length figure set on a gold coronet of thistles above a shield is St Mungo, Glasgow's patron saint, a legendary and much-loved character. The famous emblems, the fish and ring, the bird, the tree, and the bell, all of which can be traced back to ancient seals, commemorate four of the many stories about the incredible feats of Mungo.

Mungo plays such an important part in the history of Glasgow, no book on the city would be complete without mention of his colourful life. As with all great legends handed down through the generations there are several versions of the story of Mungo but the most popular is that he was born at Culross, Fife, in the early 6th century, the illegitimate son of a princess. Kentigern, as he was then known, was educated and trained as a priest of the Celtic Church at the monastery of St Serf at Culross. It was his master, St Serf, who first called him Mungo which means 'my dear friend', and the name stuck. Mungo finished his training around the year 550 and went to the house of Fergus, a holy man, at Kernach. However, the night he arrived Fergus died. It's said that Mungo put his body on a cart yoked to two wild bulls and let them take it to a place ordained by the Lord. They stopped on a steep hill above the Molendinar, one of the tributaries of the River Clyde, and this was where Fergus was buried and Mungo built a church of timber and wattle. He called the spot 'Glasgu', meaning 'dear green place' and the humble church developed into Glasgow Cathedral (*see page 45*). Mungo, who was appointed a bishop at the young age of twenty-five, lived a holy life until he died in 603. He was canonized and became the patron saint of Glasgow with a feast day on 13 January. A whole host of legends surrounds his life – this was the man who rose into the air while preaching so that the people standing at the back could see him – but the most famous are immortalized on the city's Coat of Arms.

The bird is the wild robin befriended and tamed by St Serf. It was accidentally killed one day and the blame placed on St Mungo. He took the dead bird in his arms and prayed for it to live again. The bird flew happily back to its master.

The tree is a reminder of one of Mungo's legendary feats as a young boy in the monastery. It was his responsibility to keep the holy fire in the refectory alight, but one night while he was asleep the other boys put it out. When he woke and saw the fire was no longer burning, Mungo broke off some frozen branches from a hazel tree and prayed over them. They burst into flames and the fire was rekindled.

The bell, believed to have been given to St Mungo by the Pope, was used to summon people to worship. By the 15th century 'St Mungo's Bell' was a celebrated institution in the city.

The fish with a ring in its mouth commemorates the occasion when Mungo saved the honour of Languoreth, Queen of Strathclyde. She had given the ring, a present from her husband, to a lover who lost it in the River Clyde while they were bathing one day. The jealous king, suspecting something was amiss, demanded to see the ring. Languoreth confessed her plight to Mungo who sent one of his monks to fish in the river and asked that the first fish caught be brought back to him. This fish had the ring in its mouth.

Glasgow's Motto

The city's motto, 'Let Glasgow Flourish', is a shortened version of the text written on the bell of the Tron Church cast in 1631. In full, the motto is, 'Lord, let Glasgow flourish through the preaching of Thy word and praising Thy name.'

CHAPTER ONE

Events, Entertainments and Activities

AIRDRIE OBSERVATORY, Airdrie Library, Wellwynd, Airdrie. Tel: Airdrie 63221

Observing the night sky can be great fun, but few people get the opportunity to observe it closely through a powerful telescope. And that's the particularly good thing about Airdrie Observatory; it's there for the public to use. Beginners and experts alike are welcome in this observatory which was started by pioneers during the 19th century. It houses a 6-inch (15cm) refracting telescope with a set of eye pieces which produce magnifications from 60 to 450 times. The observatory's dome is motor driven and the slit can be opened to reveal any part of the sky. A visit is certainly an experience not to be missed. (*See also Lectures, Astra, page 28 and Monklands, page 156*)

Open: by arrangement only; contact Airdrie Library (address as above)

EXTRA ... EXTRA ... In the nearby Town Hall (municipal buildings) you can see the old council chambers. They're typical of a small town council and provide seating for Airdrie's fifteen councillors and Lord Provost.

THE BARRAS, Gallowgate

This square mile of market stalls just west of Glasgow Cross (*see page 00*) was once described as 'the bargain basement of Europe', and indeed, it's a real hustle and bustle every weekend as people come from miles around to snap up the cut-price goods. But ask any Glaswegian about the world-famous market which dates back to Victorian days and you'll soon be told that it's more, much more, than just a collection of stalls: it's an institution. Cheap and cheerful it certainly is, even rather tacky and commercial, but Glasgow just wouldn't be the same without the constant patter, bright hoardings and friendly atmosphere of the Barras. Whether you're a market-goer or not, you should make sure you get at least a glimpse of the alleyways and covered markets, chock-a-block with barrows and bargain hunters, within the Barras complex. There are around 800 regular traders selling goods ranging from beds to buttons, videos to carpets, slippers to freshly cooked seafood. A climbing expedition to the Himalayas was once almost completely equipped with goods from the Barras! You'll also find plenty of pubs and cafés, and a variety of street entertainment. There's even a children's crèche so mothers can get down to the serious business of shopping!

Open: Saturday and Sunday, 0900–1700

EXTRA ... EXTRA ... Gallowgate, as the name suggests, was once the road leading to the gallows at the city gate.

THE BRIGGAIT, Stockwell Street. Tel: 042-552 3870

When the wholesale fish market moved to join the fruit

and vegetable market at Blochairn in 1976, there were plans to demolish the huge, two-tier, cast-iron, Victorian trading hall overlooking the River Clyde (*see page 125*). But luckily a new use was found – it was refurbished and opened in 1986 as a shopping and commercial centre. There are fifty permanent shops, all lovely places to browse, with interesting and specialist goods such as designer knitwear and continental confectionery on sale, a number of more traditional market stalls, several snack-bars and a continental-style cafe-theatre. Decked out with colourful banners, plants and trees, it's at its liveliest during the weekend when you can always be sure of buskers to add to the atmosphere and provide all sorts of free entertainment from puppet shows to dance routines while you shop. (*See also the Merchants' Steeple, page 55, and walk 2*)

Open: Monday–Saturday (closed Tuesday), 0930–1800; Sunday, 1100–1700

EXTRA . . . EXTRA . . . Just around the corner in Shipbank Lane is a very different kind of market, Paddy's Market. Set up by Irish immigrants in the mid-19th century as a way of earning a crust, it is full of second-hand junk and old clothes.

BONFIRE NIGHT SPECTACULAR, Glasgow Green

Remember, remember . . . the sparkling firework display held every year on Glasgow Green (*see page 112*) The skies are a blaze of colour as rockets zoom heavenwards leaving a trail of bright cascades, and Catherine wheels turn in never-ending circles creating a glow of beautiful light. It's a popular event attracting big crowds, so why not wrap up warm and join in the firework fun!

Date: 5 November
Time: 1930
Further information from: the Recreation Section, Parks and Recreation Department, 20 Trongate, Glasgow G1 5ES. Tel: 041-227 5116

EXTRA . . . EXTRA . . . Something else worth noting is the Greater Glasgow Tourist Board's monthly newspaper 'Arrival'. Full of tourist information, it also contains an up-to-date listing of what's on in the Greater Glasgow area.

CANDLERIGGS MARKET AND THE MERCHANT CITY

You'll often hear Glaswegians refer to the Merchant City. This is the area to the south and west of George Square around Ingram Street, Virginia Street and Brunswick Street. It was here, during the 18th century that wealthy traders and 'tobacco lords' transformed the streets from cattle-grazing to a busy trade centre with manufacturing, warehousing and residential areas. The Merchant City increased in prosperity and popularity during the 19th century but changes in trading patterns brought about its decline more recently – even the once-lively fruit market moved from Candleriggs in 1969 to its new site at Blochairn leaving a huge gap. However, the past few years have seen a concerted and successful effort to bring life back into the Merchant City. There's now a general weekend market at the old Candleriggs site selling everything from old clothes to new potatoes, and the area abounds with modern housing, shopping arcades, interesting boutiques and inviting coffee shops and restaurants. It's a fascinating place to wander around, full of character and atmosphere, especially at the weekend when the cries of the market traders help recall its past. (*See also Glasgow Cross page 49 and walk 2*)

EXTRA . . . EXTRA . . . Candleriggs takes its name from an 18th-century candleworks which stood in the street. Just opposite the original works there's now a specialist candleshop, The Candle Rig (111 Candleriggs. Tel 041-552 7371. Open: Monday–Saturday 1000–1730, Sunday 1200–1700). It's worth popping in to enjoy the olde-worlde interior and amazing selection of candles and accessories.

DEMONSTRATION GARDEN OPEN DAY
Demonstration Garden, Pollok Country Park.
Tel: 041-632 9299

There's music, entertainments and a barbecue each year in the Demonstration Garden (*see page 123*) in Pollok Country Park (*see page 121*) and you don't have to be a gardening enthusiast to enjoy the fun. (*See also walk 4*)

Date: First Saturday in August, but telephone to check details

EXTRA . . . EXTRA . . . For another fun day out, make for the Gala Day on the Clyde Walkway (*see Custom House Quay Gardens page 105*), held in August every year. For details contact the Recreation Section, Parks and Recreation Department, 20 Trongate, Glasgow G1 5ES. Tel: 041-227 5116.

THE GARRET MASK AND PUPPET CENTRE, 39B Otago Street. Tel: 041-339 6185

Puppets and masks have lives of their own – but if you're an enthusiast you'll already know that! Housed in The Garret is the biggest collection of puppets to be found anywhere in Scotland including ones from the first ever puppet theatre built in the United Kingdom (1951).

Open: the centre organizes a number of free events during the year – telephone for details

EXTRA . . . EXTRA . . . The centre has a specialist library which contains over 1,000 books on puppetry and related arts.

GLASGOW CARNIVAL, Fleshers' Haugh, Glasgow Green

The annual carnival is an age-old Glasgow custom dating back over 800 years to the 12th century when Bishop Jocelyn persuaded the king, William the Lion, to hold a fair every year. It's changed a lot since the days of dancing bears and sellers of holy relics, but one thing's for sure: the merrymaking still continues with side-shows, rifle ranges, candy-floss stalls and coconut shies. Obviously you have to pay to have a go on the amusements but you can go along and soak up the atmosphere of one of Glasgow's ancient traditions entirely free.

Date: last fortnight in July
Further information from: the Recreation Section, Parks and Recreation Department, 20 Trongate, Glasgow G1 5ES. Tel: 041-227 5116

EXTRA . . . EXTRA . . . In the 18th and 19th centuries the fair was often the scene of riots. In 1791 and during the 1820s special constables had to be called in to break up the fighting. Thankfully, it's altogether much friendlier today!

GLASGOW CYCLING GRAND PRIX,
Glasgow Green

Standards are always high at this, one of the city's most popular cycling competitions, so this is the event to attend to spot the new names in the cycling world and cheer them on their way to the top.

Date: mid June
Further information from: the Recreation Section, Parks and Recreation Department, 20 Trongate, Glasgow G1 5ES. Tel: 041-227 5116

EXTRA . . . EXTRA . . . If you've got your own bicycle, or plan to hire one for a day, why not follow the

15-mile (24km) cycle route through some of Glasgow's lovely parks starting at Glasgow Green (*see page 112*) and finishing at Hogganfield Park (*see page 113*)? For details contact the Recreation Section, Parks and Recreation Department (address above).

GLASGOW MARATHON

They're off . . . Every year over 12,000 people take part in the Glasgow Marathon, one of the best-loved races in the running calendar. Crowds arrive early to cheer the runners as they leave Saltmarket and round Tron Steeple, and then everyone lines the route of 26 miles 365 yards (42.19km) around Glasgow, offering encouragement at every step. The finish is outside the gates of the People's Palace (*see page 84*) which is the perfect place for the prize-giving ceremony afterwards.

Date: September
Time: start at 0930
Further information from: the Recreation Section, Parks and Recreation Department, 20 Trongate, Glasgow G1 5ES. Tel: 041-227 5116

EXTRA . . . EXTRA . . . Saltmarket was where salt was once sold for curing the fish caught in the River Clyde (*see page 125*).

GLASGOW TRYST

'Tryst' is an old Scots word for a meeting or coming together – and that's exactly what this annual celebration of Scottish traditional music is designed to be. Pipers, folk dancers, jazz musicians and singers gather together for a week of music and dance. Some of the events are by ticket (fee) only, but many take place in the streets of the Old Merchant City (*see page 20*) and everyone is free to watch – or even take part in the different activities. The Tryst was first organized in 1985 and proved such a success, it is now an annual and much-acclaimed event.

Date: November
Further information from: the Greater Glasgow Tourist Board, 35–39 St Vincent Place, Glasgow G1 2ER. Tel: 041-227 4880

EXTRA . . . EXTRA . . . the Tryst is traditionally held in the last week of November to coincide with the feast day of Scotland's patron saint, Andrew, on 30 November.

GOETHE INSTITUT, Lower Medway Building, 74 Victoria Crescent Road. Tel: 041-334 6116

The Goethe Institut was until 1975 known as the Scottish German Centre. As early as 1963, it brought German exhibitions to Glasgow – the first exhibit was by contemporary artists working in Berlin. Today it organizes a wide range of cultural activities and many of them are free. There are exhibitions, documentaries, films and lectures. Past topics have included 'Museum Architecture in the Federal Republic' (exhibition), 'Britain and Germany: Historical Patterns of a European Relationship' (lecture), and 'Berlin Chamissoplatz' (film). For some events you do need to speak German, but there are quite a number in English. Further information is available (in English!) from the Institut.

EXTRA ... EXTRA ... If you're interested in German culture, ask to be put on the Goethe Institut's free mailing list.

GUIDED TOURS – BURRELL COLLECTION, Pollok Country Park, 2060 Pollokshaws Road. Tel: 041-649 7151

If you want to know more about art history a good way to start is by joining a free guided tour of the Burrell Collection. (*See page 71 and also walk 4*)

Times: daily – details are announced on the notice board in the courtyard

---

EXTRA ... EXTRA ... To enter the courtyard you must walk under a carved sandstone arch which came from Hornby Castle in Yorkshire and which dates from the 14th century.

INTERNATIONAL FOLK FESTIVAL, Glasgow Green

First held in 1984, the week-long folk festival gets more and more popular every year. It's a truly international event with singers and dancers from all over the world decked out in traditional costume, staging free performances on Glasgow Green (*see page 112*). The People's Palace and Winter Gardens (*see page 84*) are usually the centre of activity (providing shelter so that Glasgow rain will never stop play!), but the folk theme is echoed all over the city during the festival with pubs and clubs extending their hours.

Date: July

Further information from: the Greater Glasgow Tourist Board, 35–39 St Vincent Place, Glasgow G1 2ER. Tel: 041-227 4880

EXTRA . . . EXTRA . . . The Winter Gardens are a favourite venue for folk singers not only during the festival but throughout the whole of the summer. They play – for free – against the backdrop of flowers and plants. Other places to find singers and buskers providing free entertainment are George Square (*see page 109*) and Buchanan Street.

ISLAMIC CENTRE, Mosque Avenue, Gorbals Cross. Tel: 041-429 3132

Startlingly modern, the Islamic Centre with its distinctive dome is an unusual landmark on the south side of the River Clyde (*see page 125*). Eager to disseminate information about Islam, the centre makes visitors welcome. Some of the main teachings of Islam are explained and you'll be taken on a guided tour which includes a look at the prayer hall. This large, empty, carpeted space is oriented towards Mecca – the guide explains exactly why. If you've never been inside a mosque, this is a tour well worth joining.

Open: by arrangement only; any evening except Friday
Note: you are required to dress appropriately for your
visit. Both men and women should dress 'mod-
estly' and women should wear some sort of head
covering

EXTRA . . . EXTRA . . . In complete contrast, across
the road from the Islamic Centre stands The Citizens'
Theatre – Glasgow's famous innovative repertory theatre.

LECTURES

Free lectures are held at a variety of venues on a wide
range of topics.

Astra Astra – the association in Scotland for Research
into Astronautics – holds regular lectures at the Airdrie
Observatory (*see page 17*) so if you're interested in the
planets, this is an excellent opportunity to learn from the
experts!

Dates: contact Airdrie Library, Wellwynd, Airdrie.
Tel: Airdrie 63221

Collins Gallery University of Strathclyde, 22 Richmond
Street. Tel: 041-552 4400 Ext. 2682/2416
Free lectures are a regular event at the Collins Gallery
(*see page 73*). The lectures are run in conjunction with the
exhibitions held in this highly adaptable space and cover
a wide range of topics on the arts.

Dates: These vary; telephone the above number for
details

Gardening Talks Pollok Country Park, Pollokshaws
Road. Tel: 041-227 5065
Throughout the year there are interesting talks at Pollok
Demonstration Garden (*see page 123*). They cover a wide
range of gardening subjects of interest both to amateurs
and professionals. (*See also Pollok Country Park, page
121*)

Dates: a programme giving details, dates and times is
available on request from the Director of Parks
and Recreation, 20 Trongate, Glasgow G1 5ES.
Tel: 041-227 5060

Hunterian Art Gallery University of Glasgow, 82 Hillhead
Street. Tel: 041-330 5431
In the fully equipped lecture theatre at the Hunterian Art
Gallery (*see page 77*) you can hear talks on both the
gallery's many temporary exhibitions and its superb permanent collection which includes an outstanding selection
of works by Whistler and an extensive collection of works
by Mackintosh (*see page 52*).

Dates: these vary; telephone for details

Third Eye Centre Lectures 350 Sauchiehall Street. Tel:
041-332 7521/4
The adventurous exhibitions of contemporary art held at
the Third Eye Centre (*see page 93*) are frequently comple-
mented by lectures which are open to the public. So, if
you've seen the exhibition and want to know more, this is
your chance!

Dates: usually Saturday afternoon, but telephone for
details or check in the centre's free brochure

University of Glasgow Boyd Orr Building (Lecture Theatre 2), University Avenue. Tel: 041-339 8855

Lunch-hour lectures are held regularly at the University of Glasgow. Topics covered are varied: from 'Hormones in Cancer' to 'Lexiocography and the Computer'; from 'Glasgow's Singing Tradition' to 'Bite Marks and the Criminal'! You're certainly not expected to be an expert to attend these entertaining and informative sessions.

Dates: Tuesday 1315 (duration 50 minutes). Write for full details and programme

MAYFEST

For three weeks every May Glasgow explodes into action as the city welcomes artists from all over the world at the annual 'Mayfest'. Every available venue is taken over, from theatres and museums to works canteens and day centres – wherever a performance can be held, it is! And the variety of acts and artists is as different as the venues, with every kind of music, jazz and 'alternative' theatre. It began in 1983 and is very much a community-based festival, aiming to give everyone a share in cultural events, and now with well over 100 events on the agenda each year, it's impossible not to catch some of the enthusiasm and energy of the Mayfest.

Date: mid-May. For exact dates and more information contact: Mayfest, 46 Royal Exchange Square, Glasgow. Tel: 041-221 4911

EXTRA ... EXTRA ... Royal Exchange Square, headquarters of the Mayfest, is usually used as a throughway from Queen Street into fashionable Buchanan Street, but it's worth stopping to admire the buildings around. At the east end is The Royal Exchange, now Stirling's Library (*see page 62*), while the impressive Royal Bank of Scotland building (designed by Archibald Elliot in 1827) stands at the west end.

MITCHELL LIBRARY, North Street.
Tel: 041-221 7030

Mitchell Library is named after Stephen Mitchell, a Glasgow tobacco manufacturer, who died in 1874 leaving £67,000 'for the establishment and endowment of a large public library in Glasgow, with all the modern accessories connected with it.' He certainly wouldn't be disappointed with what he would find today. The Mitchell Library is undoubtedly the place to go if you need to know something: Scottish local history, folklore, statistics, geography – there seems to be information here on every subject. It holds a unique collection of material relating to Glasgow (floor 3) including books, newspapers, maps, manuscripts and bound volumes of many local newspapers from 1741 to the present. In the Social Sciences Department (floor 2) you can find over 400 current periodicals and there's an extensive book stock covering law, economics and education. Audio language courses are available in 65 languages (floor 5) and there are important collections of Scottish literature. The Music Department (floor 4) has both reference and lending material as well as listening points, sound-proof carrels and two pianos. All in all, there's plenty to keep you occupied, for free, for a very long time!

Open: Monday–Friday 0930–2100; Saturday 0930–1700

EXTRA **. . .** ***EXTRA*** **. . .** There are many smaller libraries in Glasgow:

Anderston, Berkeley Street	041-221 7030
Baillieston, 141 Main Street	041-771 2433
Barlanark, 80 Barlanark Road	041-771 3003
Barmulloch, 99 Rockfield Road	041-558 6185
Bridgeton, 23 Landressy Street	041-554 0217
Cambuslang, 6 Glasgow Road	041-641 3909
Cardonald, 1113 Mosspark Drive	041 882 1381
Castlemilk, 5 Dougrie Drive	041-634 2066
Cathkin, 21 Lovat Place	041-634 1249
Couper Institute, 84 Clarkston Road	041-637 1544
Darnley, 32 Glen Livet Place	041-638 7203
Dennistoun, 2a Craigpark	041-554 0055
Drumchapel, 65 Hecla Avenue	041-944 5698
Easterhouse, 5 Shandwick Street	041-771 5986
Elder Park, 228a Langlands Road	041-445 1047
Gorbals, 100 Norfolk Street	041-429 0060
Govanhill, 170 Langside Road	041-423 0335
Halfway, 211 Hamilton Road	041-641 2762
Hillhead, 348 Byres Road	041-339 7223
Hutchesontown, 27–29 Cumberland Arcade	041-429 1253
Ibrox, 1/7 Midlock Street	041-427 5831
King's Park, 275 Castlemilk Road	041-632 3739
Knightswood, 27 Dunterlie Avenue	041-959 2041
Langside, 2 Sinclair Drive	041-632 0810
Maryhill, 1508 Maryhill Road	041-946 2348
Milton, 163 Ronaldsay Street	041-772 1410
Mosspark, 35 Arran Drive	041-427 0339
Parkhead, 64 Tollcross Road	041-554 0198
Partick, 305 Dumbarton Road	041-339 1303
Pollok, 100/106 Peat Road	041-881 3540
Pollokshaws, 50/60 Shawbridge Street	041-632 3544

Pollokshields, 30 Leslie Street   041-423 1460
Possilpark, 127 Allander Street   041-336 8110
Riddrie, 1020 Cumbernauld Road   041-770 4043
Rutherglen, 163 Main Street   041-647 6453
Shettleston, 154 Wellshot Road   041-778 1221
Springboig, Hallhill Road   041-774 4067
Springburn, 179 Ayr Street   041-558 5559
Stirling's, Queen Street   041-221 1876
Temple, 350 Netherton Road   041-954 5265
Townhead, 192 Castle Street   041-552 1657
Whiteinch, 14 Victoria Park Drive South   041-959 1376
Woodside, 343 St George's Road   041-332 1808

POETRY READINGS – THIRD EYE CENTRE, 350 Sauchiehall Street. Tel: 041-332 7521/4

Poetry readings are often held in the lively and informal atmosphere of the Third Eye Centre (*see page 93*). In keeping with the centre's focus on contemporary art, the readings are by Scottish, English and international poets.

Dates: see the centre's free brochure for details or telephone the above number

EXTRA ... EXTRA ... 'Sauchiehall' means 'the willow meadow'. But the street is no longer lined with willow trees; instead there are shops and restaurants down its length.

REGATTAS

When the tides are high, you'll often find rowing boats (of the competitive sort!) out on the River Clyde (*see page 125*) practising for some of the season's regattas. One of the major events is the Eights Heads of the River Race which attracts teams from universities from all over the country. Starting from Glasgow Green (*see page 112*), the boats race along the river to Kingston Bridge. Held in March every year, it makes for a good day out for spectators. Another event worth noting is Edinburgh University's annual regatta held in May at Wyndford Loch on the Forth and Clyde Canal (*see page 107*). There's always a good turn out of more serious crews, racing along the narrow, mile-long stretch of water, plus the fun-lovers decked out in colourful costumes, brightening the scene in their jolly boats. Richmond Park (*see page 125*) is another venue for Clyde Regattas.

Dates: Eights Heads of the River Race is held in March. For exact times contact the Recreation Section, Parks and Recreation Department, 20 Trongate, Glasgow G1 5ES. Tel: 041-227 5116; Edinburgh University Regatta is held in May. For exact times contact: Edinburgh Tourist Information Centre, Waverley Market, Princes Street, Edinburgh. Tel: 031-557 2727

EXTRA . . . EXTRA . . . Huge and modern, Kingston Bridge comprises three miles of elevated roadway across the River Clyde. Built in 1970; the main span over the river is 470 feet in length.

TRIATHLONS AT HOGGANFIELD LOCH

Why do triathlon events always seem to fall on cold days? Held twice a year, with junior and senior teams taking part, the venue for this gruelling challenge is Hogganfield Loch (*see page 113*). Atheletes, highly trained and motivated, put themselves through their paces with swimming, running and canoeing races. So why not brave the less than clement climes and give them your support?

Date: usually on a Sunday in June and October. For exact times contact: the Recreation Section, Parks and Recreation Department, 20 Trongate, Glasgow G1 5ES. Tel: 041-227 5116

EXTRA ... EXTRA ... If the triathletes have inspired you to take some exercise, then pick up a free information sheet, 'Sports and Recreation Facilities', which lists all the sporting venues in the area, from the Greater Glasgow Tourist Board, 35–39 St Vincent Place, Glasgow G1 2ER. Tel: 041-227 4880.

WHIFFLET COMPUTER CENTRE, Easton Place, Coatbridge (M8, Exit 10). Tel: Coatbridge 29118

If you fancy using a computer, make for the Whifflet Computer Centre. Here you'll find a wide range of computers – IBM PC, Spectrum 128, BBC Master 128K, Amstrad PCW, Commodore 128, Astari ST – which you can use under supervision. And, if you're a beginner, there are instructors available and classes in basic programming. (*See also Monklands, page 156*)

Open: Monday and Friday, 0930–1700; Tuesday and Thursday, 1400–1930; Saturday 0930–1230

EXTRA . . . EXTRA . . . While you're in Coatbridge, take a look at the modern stained-glass windows of the council chambers. They were designed in 1985 to mark the centenary of the founding of Coatbridge. The work of John Clark, they show the history of Monklands District (*see page 156*) over the last hundred years.

CHAPTER TWO

Historic and Architectural Interest

THE ANTONINE WALL

You can still follow the line of the Antonine Wall, built in about A.D. 143 during the second Roman invasion of Scotland. But don't make the mistake of searching for the remains of a stone wall like Hadrian's Wall – this one was a turf rampart set on a stone base and fronted by a deep V-sectioned ditch, so look out for a ditch rather than a wall. The Antonine Wall ran for 37 miles from Bo'ness to Old Kilpatrick and was built as a defensive frontier, preventing the northern Caledonian tribes from raiding the Scottish Lowlands and the south. The army of the wall, which at its peak totalled up to 7,000 men, was garrisoned at forts set two miles apart and a military road ran beside the wall. The wall was only manned for around 20 years, but there's much archaelogical evidence to show the lifestyle the Roman soldiers and camp followers would have led – military carts and wagons crafted from ash and elm have been found, so too have a shrine and an altar together with leather shoes and sandals of men, women and children, as well as pottery, jewellery, coins, animal bones, cooking utensils and iron weapons. Several sections of the wall can still still be seen: at Bearsden, for example, there are remains of a bathhouse which served as a small fort; at Bar Hill (signposted from the B802), the fort was the highest on the line of the wall and recent excavations have exposed the stone-built headquarters building and granary; and at Croy Hill (off the B802 just north of Croy), you can see traces of the ditch and rampart with two beacon platforms which were used to flash messages along the wall. You'll find out more about the wall and the surviving monuments in the Hunterian Museum (*see page 78 and see also Strathkelvin, page 158*)

Open: all the time

EXTRA . . . EXTRA . . . Kirkintilloch, now a major town in Strathkelvin, was the site of a Roman fort, Caerpentulach. The name Kirkintilloch means 'the fort at the end of the ridge'.

BALDERNOCK PARISH CHURCH,
Baldernock, Strathkelvin (off A807).

This simple, unadorned church was built in 1795 on the site of the original church which dated back to the 13th century. It's a building full of interest and history wherever you look. Take the inscription in the belfry, for example, which reads '*Deo Optimo Maximo*' – 'to the best and greatest God'. This is carved on a stone said to have come from the Antonine Wall (*see page 39*). A stone stile still leads to the graveyard – a wonderful place to explore as there are so many fascinating tombstones to read. The earliest is dated 1644; others record famous parishioners such as Alexander Dunlop, who played a part in the passing of the Reform Bill in the mid-19th century, and Archibald Bulloch, great-great-grandfather of Mrs Eleanor Roosevelt. The church, graveyard and beautiful countryside around all combine to make a pleasant afternoon outing. (*See also Strathkelvin page 158)*

Open: by request to the minister, Tel: 041-212 0471.

EXTRA ... EXTRA ... Look out for the small octagonal house built at the entrance to the churchyard in 1826. This was where men would stand guard over new graves to ensure the bodies weren't stolen to be sold at the Anatomy School in Glasgow.

CENTRAL STATION, Gordon Street

Built in the 1870s, Central Station, a fine example of Victorian railway architecture, marked the arrival of the Caledonian Railway in Glasgow. Even if you haven't got a train to catch, it's worth taking a look around, especially at the ornate main entrance. Central Station Hotel, on the corner of Gordon Street and Hope Street, forms part of the station – an impressive welcome for visitors, it was designed by Sir Rowand Anderson, an Edinburgh architect, and completed in 1884. And don't forget the viaduct, an extension of the original platforms over Argyle Street built between 1899 and 1905. Commonly known as the 'Hielanmans' Umbrella', this was a popular meeting place for poor Highlanders new to the city. At one time you could stand here for hours and not hear a word of English.

Open: all the time

EXTRA ... EXTRA ... Nearby, on the corner of Union Street and Gordon Street, is an almost cathedral-like warehouse known as the Ca d'Oro building.

CITY CHAMBERS, George Square. Tel: 041-227 4017

Grand and imposing, City Chambers, home of Glasgow District Council, covers the whole of the east side of George Square (*see page 109*). The building is a joy from the outside – designed by William Young in Italian Renaissance style (1883–8) – but just wait until you're inside, it's absolutely breathtaking. So do make sure it's high on your list of priorities. A visit always takes the form of a guided tour which in theory should last around 45 minutes but usually takes longer because everyone is so fascinated! The meeting point is the loggia, or entrance hall, and it's worth arriving early to soak up the atmosphere. Built to the plan of a Roman church of the Renaissance period, the granite, marble and mosaics blend in perfect harmony. Look up to the ceiling and domes – the Venetian mosaic is made up of 1,500,000 half-inch cubes, each put in by hand. Two staircases lead from the entrance hall – one to the council chamber, the other, a grand marble stairway, to reception salons and the magnificent 110-foot-long banqueting hall. Your guide will give you a potted history and fill you in on all the architectural and historical facts as he takes you around, gradually building up the excitement until you reach the highlight and grand finale – the banqueting hall. The murals showing the progress of the city are probably the best-known features of the room, but there's also so much to take in you'll feel quite mind-boggled as you leave. (*See also Council Meetings page 138, and walk 1 George Square page 109*)

Open: tours at 1030 and 1430, Monday, Tuesday, Wednesday and Friday (subject to functions)

EXTRA . . . EXTRA . . . As you book in for a tour look at the 'Glescau' tapestry behind the desk. This was designed by contemporary artist Robert Stewart to reflect Glasgow's heritage past and present – if you can't work it out, ask your guide to explain the various facets.

CLYDESDALE BANK PLC HEAD OFFICE, 40 St Vincent Place. Tel: 041-248 7070

The head office of Clydesdale Bank is said to be one of the finest examples of Palladian architecture in Europe. It was built in 1874 to the designs of John Burnett (who was also responsible for Merchants' House and the Stock Exchange, *see page 149*). Its façade is impressive, decorated with both Tuscan and Corinthian columns, the Coat of Arms of Glasgow and various other Scottish towns, and groups of sculptures representing industry and commerce. Pass through the Venetian-style vestibule with its Palladian arches and murals by Scottish artist John Halliday which depict the city's architecture through the ages – from the ancient Cathedral (*see page 45*) to a typical Glaswegian tenement – and into the Banking Hall. Here you can see the original arcades and the magnificent stained-glass dome which rises over 50 feet (15m) above floor level.

Round the corner at 150 Buchanan Street is a six-storey extension to the bank's head office. The building is faced with a mixture of polished and matt reddish granite with reflective rose-coloured glass – so, if you cross the road and look up you will see the Tron Steeple (*see Glasgow Cross page 49*) and surrounding Victorian buildings perfectly reflected!

Open: Monday-Friday, 0930–1630

EXTRA . . . EXTRA . . . Did you know the Clydesdale Bank, the Bank of Scotland and the Royal Bank of Scotland all issue their own banknotes?

COATS OBSERVATORY, Oakshaw Road, Paisley. Tel: 041-332 0961

Built in 1883, the observatory is a distinctive building in this Oakshaw area of Paisley. Designed by John Honeyman, it is one of the earliest buildings to be planned with access specifically for disabled people – Thomas Coats was himself confined to a wheelchair. Since 1884, weather recordings have been made here and daily returns are made to the Meteorological Office of wind speed and direction, barometric pressure, hours of sunshine, extent of visibility, cloud-cover, humidity, rainfall and temperature. You can see the instrument room, orrery and then climb the ramp up to the dome which houses the telescope. (*See also Renfrew, page 157*)

Open: Monday-Friday, 0400–1700; Saturday, 1000–1300
       and 1400–1700

EXTRA . . . EXTRA . . . Tradition has it that there was a Roman castellum in Oakshaw and when you see the panoramic view the site commands of the surrounding countryside it's easy to see why. However, no conclusive evidence of a permanent Roman fortification has yet been discovered.

GLASGOW BRIDGE

Known as Jamaica Bridge, Broomielaw Bridge and Glasgow Bridge, this bridge across the River Clyde (*see page 125*) was first opened in 1772. However, within fifty years it had become quite unsuitable for the ever-increasing heavy traffic and Thomas Telford was brought in to design a new bridge. Opened in 1836, it was the widest and most spacious in Great Britain at the time. However, sixty years on, it just wasn't big enough and so it was redesigned in its present form with some of Telford's bridge built into the new structure.

Open: all the time

EXTRA . . . EXTRA . . . Next to Glasgow Bridge is the Suspension Bridge which leads pedestrians over the river to Carlton Place. Built in 1851, it has a 414-foot (126m) span with pylons in the form of triumphal arches. There's a replica of the Suspension Bridge built across the river at Glasgow Green. (*See page 112*)

GLASGOW CATHEDRAL, Castle Street.
Tel: 041-552 0220

There's so much to see inside Glasgow Cathedral that it's perhaps a good idea to begin your visit by studying its exterior. Climb the nearby necropolis (*see page 56*) and you'll gain an excellent view which clearly shows the size and plan of this ancient building. The original church was built in the early 12th century; its first stone is thought to have been consecrated in 1136 in the presence of King David I. Destroyed by fire, this small early building was succeeded by a larger one consecrated in 1197. During the 13th century the nave was extended, the quire added and the unique low church built. The west window dates from the 14th century and the pulpitum and the Blacader aisle (named after Archbishop Robert Blacader) were added in the 15th century. Descending the necropolis, enter the cathedral by its southwest door and walk to the centre of the nave – from here you can look down the whole length of the building – and begin to explore! There's plenty to discover, but try not to miss:

West Window – above the main west door. Its intricate stained glass depicts Adam and Eve surrounded by fauna and flora beneath golden rays which symbolize the light which veils the Divine Mystery.

Old Bell – northwest corner. This bell, 12 feet 1 inch (3.62m) in circumference, once hung in the now demolished bell tower. It was the gift of Gavin Dunbar, Archbishop of Glasgow (1524–47).

Scots Guards Memorial Window – northwest corner. Unveiled in 1956, the window symbolizes the four freedoms: freedom from want and fear, and freedom of speech and worship.

Painted Stone – beside the first pillar in the northwest corner. Thought to have been part of the cathedral consecrated in 1397, this wedge-shaped stone from an arch is plastered and painted on two sides.

Quire Screen – east side of the nave. Made from stone and dating from the 15th century, the quire screen almost completely hides the quire from the nave. It's the only screen of its kind left in a non-monastic church of pre-Reformation date in Scotland.

Pulpit Hour Glass – in the quire. This showed both preacher and congregation the passage of time during a sermon!

Royal Pew – south side of the chancel. For over a century there has been a royal pew in the cathedral. Today you can see two armchairs with the arms and monogram of HM The Queen and HRH The Prince Philip, Duke of Edinburgh.

Upper Chapter House – entered through a door in the northernmost ambulatory chapel. This annexe, built during the 13th century, was rebuilt during the 15th century during the time of Bishop William Lauder (1408–25) whose arms can be seen on a panel.

The Lower Church – reached from the quire by a stairway. The 'forest of columns' of the lower church, often wrongly described as the crypt, is perhaps the most intriguing part of the cathedral. Here you can see the covenanters' memorial which commemorates nine convenanters who were hanged and beheaded at Glasgow Cross (*see page 49*) in 1684. You can also see the remains of the 12th-century cathedral – a single vaulting shaft with distinctive late-12th-century decoration. Finally don't miss the tomb of St Mungo, patron saint of Glasgow (*see page 11*). During mediaeval times thousands of pilgrims made their way to this sacred spot. Indeed, in 1451 the Pope decreed that it was as meritorious to make a pilgrimage to Glasgow Cathedral as it was to visit Rome itself!

Open: October–March, Monday–Saturday, 0930–1200 and 1300–1600, Sunday, 1400–1600; April–September, Monday–Saturday, 0930–1300 and 1400–1900, Sunday 1400–1700

EXTRA . . . EXTRA . . . Regimental colours are to be found throughout the cathedral and make an interesting study in their own right. Down the nave you'll find:

South Wall (Cameron Corner) – three colours of the 26th Cameronians (1st Battalion Scottish Rifles) in a glass case.

West Wall (south to north) – two colours of 2nd Battalion Highland Light Infantry; two colours of 1st Battalion Highland Light Infantry; two colours of 1st Battalion Scots Guards.

North side of Nave (west to east) – two colours of 5th Battalion Highland Light Infantry; three colours of 17th Battalion Highland Light Infantry; two colours of 15th Battalion Highland Light Infantry.

South side of Nave (east to west) – two colours of 6th Battalion Highland Light Infantry; three colours of 18th Battalion Highland Light Infantry; three colours of 16th Battalion Highland Light Infantry.

North Transept (north wall) – two colours of 15th (Scottish) Battalion Parachute Regiment; colour of 602 City of Glasgow Auxiliary Squadron, RAF; Royal Navy; Merchant Navy.

South Transept (south wall) – Anson Battalion Royal Naval Division; Fourth Assaye colour carried first by 2nd Battalion Highland Light Infantry, then by 2nd Battalion Highland Light Infantry, lastly by Royal Highland Fusiliers; colour of Queen's Own Royal Glasgow Yeomanry.

South Transept (memorial desk) – two colours of 1st Battalion Queen's Own Cameron Highlanders.

While in the quire you can see:

Beneath Quire loft (under glass) – Colour 1st Battalion 3rd (Scots) Foot Guards.

Sacristy (Upper Chapter House) – Original Assaye colour of 74th Regiment of Foot (Highland Light Infantry); the King's and Regimental colours of 74th Regiment of foot (Highland Light Infantry).

GLASGOW CROSS

'The Cross' is the meeting point of four busy roads – High Street, Saltmarket, Gallowgate and Trongate. During the 18th century the area was known as 'The Golden Acre'; a hubbub of trading and administration where the tobacco lords, who made their fortunes in trade with the American Colonies and the West Indies, and the prosperous merchants of the city would promenade and conduct their daily business. Today, however, it is better known as a traffic throughway, rather than a stopping point, leading uphill to Glasgow Cathedral (*see above*) and down to the River Clyde (*see page 125*).

Right at the centre is the Tolbooth Steeple, erected in 1626. Standing 12 feet (3.62 m) square and 126 feet (38.4 m) high with a weathervane at the top, this tower is all that remains of the 'Town House' where the tobacco lords used to meet. It's not open to the public but to give you an idea of how the old tolbooth building used to look there's a model in the People's Palace Museum (*see page 84*). Opposite is the Mercat Cross, a 1929 replica of the old mediaeval cross. And nearby, in Trongate, is the elegant Tron Steeple forming an arch over the footpath.

Built in 1637 this is the last remains of St Mary's Church which was burnt down by the 'Hellfire Club' in 1793, and is now a flagship for the Glasgow Tron Theatre Club which has its premises at the rear. An important and busy junction in the city (it seems that all roads lead to The Cross!), the area is well worth exploring – and not just from the top of a bus!

Open: all the time

EXTRA . . . EXTRA . . . It was near the Tolbooth Steeple that the first pavement or 'Plainstaines' was laid in Glasgow.

HUTCHESONS' HALL, 158 Ingram Street (corner of John Street). Tel: 041-552 8391

Stand at the far end of Hutcheson Street for the best view of this spired building designed by David Hamilton between 1802 and 1805. It's now owned by the National Trust for Scotland and is a visitor centre, shop and regional office, but it was originally built as a new home for a charitable hospital and school. The charity which was first housed in Trongate was founded in 1641 by two brothers: George Hutcheson (1558–1639) who left money for a hospital for 'aged decrepit men of the age of above 50 years – known to be destitute of all help and support – being merchants, craftsmen or any other trade without distinction', and Thomas Hutcheson (1590–1641) who bequeathed funds for 'educating and harbouring twelve male children, indigent orphans or others of the like condition and quality'. Their statues, the work of James

Colquhoun, were moved from the original building and now stand proudly in niches at the first-floor level. Inside, the memory of the two benevolent brothers lives on in tiny and touching details throughout. Do ask to see the impressive hall upstairs which is often used for small exhibitions, displays and special functions. (*See also walk 2*)

Open: Monday–Friday, 0900–1700

EXTRA . . . EXTRA . . . There are lots of free leaflets about places of interest in and around Glasgow in the foyer.

KIRK O'SHOTTS PARISH CHURCH,
Salsburgh (M8, Exit 5)

Kirk O'Shotts parish church, dramatically situated on a hill 1,000 feet (305m) above sea level, is built on the site of a mediaeval chapel. During its heyday in the 19th century, 'hell-fire' preachers speaking here attracted a large congregation, many of whom walked from the neighbouring village of Airdrie (*see Monklands, page 157*). Today's visitors are attracted not to the church, but to its spectacular graveyard which sweeps down the steep hillside to the busy M8 and which contains a number of evocative covenanters' tombs. If you can, pay a visit in winter when the surrounding landscape is starkly beautiful. (*See also Monklands, page 156*)

Open: cemetery daily until dusk; church open by appointment

EXTRA . . . EXTRA . . . The village of Salsburgh dates back to 1726 when records show just four houses.

CHARLES RENNIE MACKINTOSH

Charles Rennie Mackintosh, an important figure in the history of modern architecture, is regarded as one of Glasgow's most famous sons. And it's here in his native city that you can see many of his most interesting and influential buildings which are listed below. The most fascinating of all, Glasgow School of Art in Renfrew Street, makes a small charge for an internal tour, but you can view its impressive façade with imaginative wrought-iron work from the outside. Where opening times are given, entrance is possible and free.

Queen's Cross Church, 870 Garscube Road.
Tel: 041-946 6600
Now the headquarters of the Charles Rennie Mackintosh Society, Queen's Cross is the best place to start your tour of Mackintosh buildings. Here you can pick up information about the architect's life and work. The church itself (built 1897–9) is a sturdy building on a cramped site. However, its interior seems both grand and spacious and most definitely retains the flavour of Mackintosh.

Open: Tuesday, Thursday, Friday, 1200–1730; Sunday, 1430–1700

Glasgow Herald Building, corner of Mitchell Street and Mitchell Lane
Erected between 1893 and 1895, this building shows early

evidence of Mackintosh's distinct style – look out for the carved stone and wrought-iron ornamentation.

Martyrs Public School, Parson Street
The basic symmetry of Martyrs is the result of the educational segregation of the sexes which was the order of the day. Despite restraints from his client, Mackintosh's individuality is very evident.

Ruchill Church Hall, 24 Ruchill Street
It's good to see a community building so frequently used and it clearly shows how hardy Mackintosh's designs have proved to be. His 'signature' in wood and glass is apparent in this hall which vibrates with the activities of youth organizations, pensioners' groups and church functions.

Open: by arrangement Tuesday, Wednesday, Thursday, 1030–1530

Daily Record Building, Renfield Lane
This impressive façade which dates from 1901, the year of Glasgow's great international exhibition, is difficult to view as Renfield Lane is very narrow. However, do risk cricking your neck because the glazed white-and-green brickwork towering some four storeys high is an attractive sight.

Willow Tea Room, 217 Sauchiehall Street
You can buy a cup of tea here (but the manageress doesn't mind Mackintosh enthusiasts peeking through the doorway) and relax in the opulence of Edwardian Glasgow. Both the interior and the exterior were designed by Mackintosh in 1903 and have now been restored (using original drawings and surviving fittings) to their original purpose.

Open: Monday–Saturday, 0930–1630. Tel: 041-332 0521

Scotland Street School, 225 Scotland Street.
Tel: 041-429 1202
Designed and built in 1904, during Mackintosh's most active period, Scotland Street School has the full stamp of the Mackintosh style, and it's delightful! Look out particularly for the north façade which is dominated by staircase bays made almost entirely of glass. (*See also Scotland Street School Museum of Education, page 90*)

Open: Monday–Friday, 1030–1230, 1330–1600
For more information on all the above buildings contact:
Charles Rennie Mackintosh Society, Queen's Cross, 870 Garscube Road, Glasgow G20. Tel: 041-946 6600. (*See also Hunterian Art Gallery (Mackintosh House), page 77, Kelvingrove Gallery, page 79; walk 3*)

EXTRA . . . EXTRA . . . If after visiting some of the above buildings you've become a Mackintosh fan, you might like to know a few more dates associated with his life and work in Glasgow:

1868 Born 7 June in Glasgow
1884 Began professional training with John Hutchison. Started attending evening classes at Glasgow School of Art
1889 Joined architects Honeyman and Keppie, Glasgow
1891 Awarded travelling scholarship to Italy
1893–4 Designed alterations to entrance hall and library of Craigie Hall, Glasgow
1896 Glasgow School of Art competition
1897 Designed furniture for the Argyle Street Tea Rooms
1898 Project for Glasgow International Exhibition

1898–9 Made extension to office premises at 233 Vincent Street
1900 Designed interior and furniture for his own flat at 120 Mains Street
1904 Made partner in architectural firm – Honeyman, Keppie and Mackintosh
1906 Moved to 78 Southpark Avenue where he designed exterior and interior alterations. Redesigned Glasgow School of Art west wing
1907 Designed the Oak Room, Ingram Street Tea Rooms, Glasgow
1914 Left Glasgow and moved to Walberswick in Suffolk
1928 Died 10 December in London

THE MERCHANTS' STEEPLE, Bridgegate

Rising from the midst of The Briggait (*see page 18*), the 'Bri'gate Steeple' a grade A listed monument, is all that survives from the Merchants' Hall of 1651–9. The steeple, which was used as a lookout for ships arriving up the River Clyde (*see page 125*), rises to a height of 164 feet (50m) with four square towers of diminishing dimensions. The ship in full sail, a symbol of Glasgow's trading origins, is mirrored on the new Merchants' House (*see page 163*) which was completed in 1877.

Open: viewing from the outside only at all times

EXTRA . . . EXTRA . . . The Bridgegate was once a fashionable street leading to the city's first stone bridge (built in 1345), the earliest crossing the River Clyde.

NECROPOLIS, Castle Street

Tucked away behind Glasgow Cathedral (*see page 45*), the necropolis is a great place to take a windy walk in the middle of the city. As you follow the path winding up through the splendid and very well kept 19th-century tombstones – thousands of them – the traffic below seems to get noisier. And, at the very top, you can hear the sound of planes and factories as well as cars and buses because over the top of the hill lies industrial Glasgow. Indeed, from the summit of the necropolis there's a spectacular view of both the domestic and the working faces of the city. While you're on the brow of the hill take the opportunity to pay a visit to the impressive monument built to the memory of John Knox (c. 1514–72). The stern figure of this eminent person in the history of the Scottish Kirk – the man who spearheaded Protestant Reformation in Scotland – can't be missed, standing on the top of a high, classical column.

Open: Monday–Saturday, 0900–2000; Sunday, 0900–1600

EXTRA . . . EXTRA . . . The streets of 18th-century Glasgow were prowled by 'promulgators' – Calvinists who imposed a ten o'clock curfew on the city. It is thought by some that the nursery rhyme 'Wee Willie Winkie' may be a witty satire about their restrictive activities:

> Wee Willie Winkie
> Runs through the toon;
> Upstairs and doonstairs
> In his nicht goon;

Chappin' at the windae
Tirlin' at the lock;
Are a' bairnies in their beds?
It's past ten o'clock.

Anyway, the laureate of the jingle, William Miller, died on 20 August 1872 and you can see his commemorative stone in the necropolis.

ORR SQUARE CHURCH, Orr Square, Paisley. Tel: 041-889 3151

It's sometimes difficult to obtain entry into the church but even if you only view it from the outside there's plenty to see, as Orr Square is itself worth visiting. The square was once the site of the town's first hospital (built in 1618) known as 'Wee Steeple' and which was run as an alms-house. The present square was laid out in 1808 and the church with its distinctive Romanesque Revival style dates from 1845. (*See also Renfrew, page 157*)

Open: by appointment only

EXTRA ... EXTRA ... Walk up Orr Street, a narrow, cobbled lane, and you'll come to Hutchenson's Charity School (corner of Orr Street and Oakshaw Street). It was established by Margaret Hutchenson at the beginning of the 19th century for the instruction of orphans and poor children.

PAISLEY ABBEY, Abbey Close, Paisley.
Tel: 041-889 3630

Known as the birthplace of the Stewart dynasty, Paisley Abbey was founded in 1163 by the High Steward of Scotland, Walter Fitzalan, but in 1307 it was burned down by the English army. You can still see some small parts of the 12th-century building but most of the present abbey dates back to the 14th century when it was restored; the second phase of restoration began in 1853 but was not finished until 1928. Today the abbey's regimental flags, relics and beautiful stained glass make it an atmospheric and popular tourist attraction for Paisley. (*See also Renfrew, page 157*)

Open: Monday–Saturday, 1000–1200 and 1300–1500

EXTRA . . . EXTRA . . . Beside the abbey you'll find Place of Paisley – an ancient complex of domestic buildings associated with the abbey and the only example of its kind in Scotland. Incidentally, 'Place' is a corruption of the word 'Palace'.

ST ANDREW'S PARISH CHURCH, St Andrew's Square. Tel: 041-560 3280

One of the few surviving architectural reminders of the wealth and glory of Glasgow's tobacco lords, this fine Georgian church was completed in 1756 to the designs of Allan Dreghorn with Mungo Naismyth as master mason. Set in the centre of a square, a pattern of building that soon became popular in Glasgow, it is modelled on London's St Martin-in-the-Fields, although the tall, thin steeple gives it a truly Scottish stamp. The interior is quite magnificent with rococo plasterwork and mahogany gallery fronts.

Open: Wednesday, Friday and Sunday, 1100–1200, or by arrangement

---

EXTRA . . . EXTRA . . . Nearby, in Turnbull Street, is the now disused St Andrew's-by-the-Green Church, built in 1751. For many years it was the only church in Glasgow with an organ and was given the nickname 'The Whistlin' Kirk'. It is now being restored for use as offices.

ST ANDREW'S ROMAN CATHOLIC CATHEDRAL, 172 Clyde Street.
Tel: 041-221 3096

Overlooking the River Clyde (*see page 000*), the recently restored St Andrew's Roman Catholic Cathedral was designed by J. Gillespie Graham and built in 1816. One of the earliest examples of Gothic Revival in Glasgow, it cost £16,000, a huge amount at the time. It's worth crossing the road to admire the 'college chapel' front, then walk around inside and enjoy the beautiful plaster-vaulted interior. All visitors are welcome, but do respect that this is a house of prayer and keep your silence. (*See also walk 2*)

Open: Monday–Friday, 0700–1800

EXTRA . . . EXTRA . . . Nearby is St Enoch Square, now a busy travel centre with bus and underground stations and an information office. 'Enoch' is a corruption of 'Thenew', the name of St Mungo's mother.

ST DAVID'S 'RAMSHORN' CHURCH, 98 Ingram Street. Tel: 041-552 4400

Why Ramshorn? Well, no one is quite sure, although there is a theory that this impressive church was named after a monastery which once stood on the site. However, there is more solid evidence to show that it was built in 1824 to the designs of Thomas Rickman, a one-time doctor of medicine, who despite being a Quaker himself worked on churches of different denominations. Well positioned at the northern end of Candleriggs (*see page 20*), it is a good example of the revival of Early Decorated Style.

Open: daily

EXTRA . . . EXTRA . . . Take a close look at the pavement outside the church. This used to be part of the cemetery and engraved in a paving slab are the initials R.F. and A.F. This marks the grave of the Foulis brothers, celebrated 18th-century printers.

ST GEORGE'S TRON CHURCH, Buchanan Street

Dominating Nelson Mandela Place (formerly St George's Place), this impressive church was designed by William Stark and built in 1807 to replace the Old Wynd Church in Trongate. The main feature is its tower, which was inspired by the work of Sir Christopher Wren. Look upwards to the obelisks surrounding the clock – apparently, it was originally proposed that these should be statues of the four evangelists. (*See also walk 1*)

Open: daily

EXTRA ... EXTRA ... The building on the north side of the Place was designed by John Burnet in 1888. The four stone figures are Reynolds, Wren, Purcell and Flaxman.

ST VINCENT STREET FREE CHURCH,
265 St Vincent Street. Tel: 041-954 4482

Standing at the top end of St Vincent Street, this temple-like church, completed in 1859, is built on a high podium, its rather strange-looking tower rising above the surrounding buildings. It was designed by the famous Glasgow architect Alexander 'Greek' Thomson, who as his nickname suggests had a passion for the Classical style of Ancient Greece. The classical emphasis is most strongly felt in the end elevations of the church – elsewhere it's a mixture of styles and a showcase of Thomson's innovative genius. Internally, there's a feeling of space and light, and the design is so imaginative you find your eyes darting from one detail to the next. Look out especially for the decorative plant and shellfish motifs which were so characteristic of Thomson, but rather remarkably flamboyant for a Presbyterian sanctuary. The church is a friendly and welcoming place to visit and the best time to look around is just before a service. The times are listed outside. (*See also walk 7*)

Open: telephone to check hours

EXTRA . . . EXTRA . . . The Greek style of which Thomson was so fond could be expressed well in dark-grey Scottish stone because it is easily mistaken for marble. A good example are the columns in the entrance hall of City Chambers (*see page 42*).

STIRLING'S LIBRARY, Queen Street.
Tel: 041-221 1876

A statue of the Duke of Wellington on his favourite charger, Copenhagen, welcomes you to the magnificent Royal Exchange building, now home of Stirling's Library. It is the central lending library for the city with around 40,000 books on the shelves, but the building, one of the few remaining in Glasgow from the Georgian period, is of great historical and architectural importance. It started life in 1780 as a mansion for William Cunningham, one of the city's tobacco lords, but was later occupied by the Royal Bank of Scotland and then in 1829 opened as the Royal Exchange. In keeping with its new role as the meeting place for the businessmen of the city, a great hall was added at the rear and a massive Corinthian portico surmounted by a clock tower was designed by David Hamilton as a grand entrance. However, the Cunningham mansion with its elegant balustrades and graceful plaster-work remained at the heart of the building and the tremendous wealth of its first owner is still very much in evidence. The beautiful elliptical hall, now the Lending Library, was once the ballroom and is a study in opulence. The main feature is the 30-foot (9m) barrel-vaulted roof supported by monolithic pillars. Chandeliers catch the light and show off the richly coffered ceiling in its full glory. The information plaques in the entrance hall explain more of the history and make interesting reading.

Open: Monday, Tuesday, Thursday and Friday, 0930–2000; Saturday, 0930–1300, 1400–1700

EXTRA . . . EXTRA . . . Among the distinguished guests to be entertained here in the past were Dickens, Gladstone and Disraeli, so you're following in famous footsteps!

TEMPLETON'S CARPET FACTORY, off Glasgow Green.

You're not seeing things! This ornate Victorian factory really is modelled on the Doge's Palace in Venice. The reason? Well, when the famous carpet manufacturers, James Templeton and Co, proposed a factory on the site in the 1880s, the City Fathers decided that as it was so near to the much-treasured Glasgow Green (*see page 112*), it had to be a truly beautiful building. Templeton nominated William Leiper as the architect and Leiper chose one of his favourite buildings, the Doge's Palace, as his theme. Elaborately decorated with coloured, glazed brick, battlements, arches and pointed windows, it is a most intriguing sight so near to the city centre. The factory, which produced carpets for royal weddings and christenings and covered many a famous floor, closed in 1979 and the building is now used as offices for small businesses.

Open: viewing from outside only, all the time

EXTRA . . . EXTRA . . . The brickwork of the building is of such high quality that apprentice bricklayers often come here to study and learn from it.

THOMAS COATS MEMORIAL BAPTIST CHURCH, High Street, Paisley.
Tel: 041-889 9980

Whatever you do, make sure you visit this splendid church on any trip you make to Paisley. Its barrelled roof is an unusual sight in Scotland and the extraordinarily lavish woodcarving (note particularly the oak screens and canopies in the transepts) is well worth close examination. Take a good look at the floor level too; the mosaics, made from 350,000 pieces of coloured marble which show the lamb and four evangelists are beautiful. The church, Gothic in design, is considered to be the masterpiece of the architect Hippolyte Blanc (1844–1917) and has been classed as one of the finest Nonconformist buildings in Europe. (*See also Renfrew, page 157*)

Open: Due to vandalism the church can't be left open unattended so it is best to telephone in advance for opening times

---

EXTRA . . . EXTRA . . . Look out for the letter 'C' incorporated into the design of many of the decorative features of the church. It stands for Thomas Coats (1809–83) who was one of the first laymen to be elected President of the Baptist Union of Scotland. The church was commissioned by the Coats family in memory of their father.

THE TRADES HOUSE, 85 Glassford Street

The mosaic pavement outside the entrance leaves you in no doubt where you are – this is Trades House, home of the 14 incorporated trades of Glasgow. Designed by Robert Adam in 1794, the façade is still almost completely intact; cross over the road to admire it fully. The hall, the oldest secular building in the city still used for its original purpose, is often host to various functions, but if there's no sign of activity then you're free to take a look around the magnificent interior, enjoying the elaborate carvings, stained-glass windows and other fine details. The banqueting hall, panelled in Spanish mahogany, is reached through an ornate doorway at the top of the main staircase. A feature of the room is the silk frieze made in Belgium in the 19th century which shows the 14 different crafts at work. Starting from the east wall, make your way around from left to right – first the tailors, then the hammermen (the goldsmiths, silversmiths, blacksmiths, saddlers and shipbuilders), next the wrights (carpenters and joiners), then the coopers or barrel-makers. On the south wall you can see the fleshers (butchers) and masons with the tools of their trade; and on the west wall, the gardeners, barbers, dyers, skinners (leather-workers and furriers), bakers and weavers. The north wall is occupied by the maltmen, known today as brewers and distillers, and the cordiners (shoemakers). Other rooms open to the public are the saloon with its white marble Adam fireplace and the reception room downstairs. Created out of a former spirit shop in the 1930s, this room boasts a splendid Adam-style ceiling and three most fascinating oak chairs – take a look at the inscriptions. (*See also walk 2*)

Open: Monday–Friday, 1000–1700

EXTRA . . . EXTRA . . . Above the fireplace in the reception room you'll find framed copies of the original design drawings for the house.

CHAPTER THREE
Museums, Galleries and Collections

THE AULD KIRK MUSEUM, Cowgate, Kirkintilloch (off A803). Tel: 041-775 1185

The Auld Kirk, one of the oldest surviving buildings in Kirkintilloch, was built in 1644 as the new parish church – and you can still see the datestone on the south gable. Full of atmosphere and historic interest, it has been renovated and refurbished and is now home for a changing programme of special exhibitions with themes as diverse as local pottery, football and wild cats! While you are here, do take a look around the churchyard with its fascinating gravestones including one of an 18th-century stonemason inscribed with sketches of the tools of his trade. Next door is the Barony Chambers Museum. (*See page 70*). (*See also Strathkelvin, page 158*)

Open: Tuesday, Thursday and Friday, 1400–1700; Saturday, 1000–1300, 1400–1700

EXTRA . . . EXTRA . . . You can still see the remains of the iron rings (known as 'jougs') which were once on the wall by the front door. This was where local offenders were tied while the congregation gathered inside the church.

THE BARONY CHAMBERS MUSEUM, The Cross, Kirkintilloch (off A803).
Tel: 041-775 1185

There's a homely, welcoming feel to this museum of local life. Although the premises are small, plenty of imagination has been used to make sure the exhibits are as lively and interesting as possible. Of particular appeal is the reconstruction of the 'single end' showing what life was like in a working-class home earlier this century. An old woman sits mending by gas light, a baby sleeps in a wooden cradle and all around are authentic items – an oatmeal crusher, flat iron, box bed, 'crystal' radio set . . . you can stand and stare at it for ages. However, the museum also highlights the rise and fall of local industries, such as weaving, coalmining and boatbuilding and the influence of the Forth and Clyde Canal (*see page 107*) and Edinburgh and Glasgow Railway on the area, as well as displaying many other items of interest. In fact, it's hard to believe so much can be fitted into such a little space! Opposite, and worth combining with your visit, is the Auld Kirk (*see above*). (*See also Strathkelvin page 158*)

Open: Tuesday, Thursday and Friday, 1400–1700; Saturday, 1000–1300, 1400–1700

EXTRA . . . EXTRA . . . The building which houses the museum was built in 1814 to 1815. The ground floor was originally a jail. The middle floor was used as the town hall and council chambers while the top floor was a rather cramped school known as the 'Steeple School'.

BURRELL COLLECTION, Pollok Country Park, 2060 Pollokshaws Road.
Tel: 041-649 7151

A purpose-built space in a beautiful landscape, containing an outstanding collection – that's the Burrell! The combination of excellent works of art presented in exactly the right architectural setting, is, quite simply, stunning. The Burrell Collection is perhaps the most impressive gallery in Britain and it certainly ranks amongst the best in Europe. Each exhibit is precisely presented to show it off to the full – take a look at the figure of à Lohan. This chinese statue, which is from the Ming Dynasty, is situated in front of a wall of glass behind which you can see the dappled woodland of Pollok Country Park (*see page 121*). Its stoneware with polychrome on biscuit glaze (which still has traces of original gilding) positively glows during the autumn when its leafy backdrop changes colour to shades of burnt orange and brown. By contrast, the period rooms create the impression of homely interiors like the oak-panelled Gothic domestic room with its tapestries of David and Bathsheba and furniture which includes a Netherlandish armoire. Then there's Islamic metalwork and ceramics – artifacts from the 9th to the 17th centuries including examples of 12th- and 13th-century Persian fritware. And don't miss the painting gallery where you can see fine works by Cranach, Memling, Bellini, Delacroix, Corbet, Renoir, Cézanne and many, many, others. It's impossible to describe all there is to see in the Burrell Collection; suffice, then, to say do make a visit! (*See also walk 4 and guided tours, page 26*)

Open: Monday–Saturday, 1000–1700; Sunday, 1400–1700

EXTRA . . . EXTRA . . . The collection once belonged to one man, William Burrell, an intensely private individual who believed 'the collection not the collector is the important thing'. Nevertheless, it is interesting to note some of the main events in his life. Born in 1861, William took over the family firm of Burrell & Son on the death of his father in 1885. He soon began collecting works of art, carefully recording his acquisitions in purchase books, and in 1923 he was appointed trustee of the National Galleries of Scotland. In 1927 he was knighted for his services to art in Scotland and was appointed trustee of the National Gallery of British Art (which is now known as the Tate Gallery). In 1944, Sir William Burrell donated his personal collection to the city of Glasgow and between 1944 and 1948 he gave Glasgow £450,000 to provide a gallery for the works. However, it wasn't until 1983 that the Burrell Collection was opened by Her Majesty the Queen, and its architect, Barry Gasson, was awarded a gold medal for architecture by the Royal Scottish Academy.

CLYDEBANK DISTRICT MUSEUM, Old Town Hall, Clydebank (off A82). Tel: 041-952 1416

Clydebank is probably best known for the famous vessels launched from local yards including *Queen Elizabeth II*, *Ramillies* and *Empress of Britain*, and this museum of local history traces the development of the shipyards and has many ship models on show. There are also displays on early pre-Roman settlements in the area and the

Roman occupation by the soldiers who built the Antonine Wall (*see page 39*). But of all the exhibits, you can't help but be drawn towards the collection of sewing machines and sewing memorabilia. These are a lasting reminder of the now closed-down Kiltowie factory, opened by the Singer Manufacturing Company in 1884 and at the time the largest in Europe.

Open: Monday and Wednesday, 1400–1700; Saturday, 1000–1700

EXTRA . . . EXTRA . . . The nearby town of Old Kilpatrick is said to be the birthplace of St Patrick.

COLLINS GALLERY, University of Strathclyde, 22 Richmond Street. Tel: 041-552 4400 ext 2682/2416

The Collins Gallery is a small, adaptable space which belongs to the University of Strathclyde. Situated on the university campus, it provides a stimulating focus for the Arts. The varied programme of temporary exhibitions and related events includes fine and applied art, architecture, photography, local history, theatre and music.

Open: (during exhibitions only; telephone for details) Monday–Friday, 1000–1700; Saturday, 1200–1600

EXTRA . . . EXTRA . . . the University of Strathclyde came into being in 1796 when it was called Anderson's Institute after Professor John Anderson who held the chair of Natural Philosophy at Glasgow University. It now has some 7000 students.

COMPASS GALLERY, 178 West Regent Street. Tel: 041-221 6370

This, the oldest contemporary art gallery in Glasgow, opened during the 1960s. It is a small non-profitmaking enterprise which really encourages people to browse around its exhibits (of course, you're also most welcome to buy the works of art on show!). The gallery promotes a blend of abstract and figurative art, but it certainly remains open to other new trends. If you can visit at Christmastime you're in for a real treat as Compass hosts an extravaganza with a huge range of exhibits. During the summer season there's a chance to see what the year's art school graduates have been working at. But any time of year you can be sure of a welcome in this friendly gallery.

Open: Monday–Saturday, 1000–1730

EXTRA . . . EXTRA . . . Compass Gallery publishes a regular and highly informative newsletter which, if you're interested, you can receive each month.

COUNTRYSIDE RANGER CENTRE, Pollok Country Park, Pollokshaws Road. Tel: 041-632 9299

The Ranger Service belongs to Pollok Country Park (*see page 121*) and inside its small visitors' centre you can see displays about the park and its extensive wildlife. The centre is a good place to pick up information; posters give the latest news of forthcoming events in the park, and there are all sorts of leaflets outlining nature trails. Free Ranger-led guided walks are available all year round (telephone in advance for details). Lasting about 1½ hours they provide an excellent introduction to the world of nature including the flowers, trees, birds and pond life which can be found in the park together with the history of the estate. The Ranger Service can also tell you about Countryside Rovers Week which takes place during August each year. (*See also walk 4*)

Open: times vary, so telephone in advance

EXTRA . . . EXTRA . . . The centre is situated in the Old Stable Courtyard of Pollok House (*see page 85*) and nearby you can see the original water-powered sawmill which is thought to date from 1880. Here timber was sawn until World War II. The first wheel was, however, replaced long ago in 1890 by a much more efficient turbine which also provided electricity for the house.

GLASGOW ARTS CENTRE, 12 Washington Street. Tel: 041-221 4526

Participation is very much the name of the game at the Glasgow Arts Centre. The idea is to give everyone of all ages, backgrounds and abilities the opportunity to take part in and enjoy the arts in their various shapes and forms whether it be dance, photography or folk music. The centre holds teaching sessions, workshops, exhibitions and special events, many of which are free, all designed to get people to join in, voice their opinions and, who knows, maybe discover some latent talent! The atmosphere is informal and enthusiastic, but be warned: this is not for the shy or faint-hearted. There's no sitting on the sidelines: when they say everyone takes part in activities, they mean it!

Open: for details of dates and further information call in at the office (address above) Monday–Friday, 0900–1645, or write, enclosing a large SAE, for a free brochure

---

EXTRA . . . EXTRA . . . A short walk away in Hope Street is the the Theatre Royal, now the home of Scottish opera. Many of the world's finest singers, musicians and actors have performed here, although legend has it that a ghost haunts the building!

HAGGS CASTLE MUSEUM, 100 St Andrew's Drive, Pollokshields. Tel: 041-427 2725

If you arrive with a child you'll be sure of a warm welcome, because this museum has been designed specifically for children and there's certainly plenty for them to see and do! There's a treasure trail to follow through a series of period rooms, clothes to dress up in, and musical instruments to play. And that's if you're unexpected – if you book in advance there's even more! A typical range of exciting activities for children includes dancing, candle-making, weaving, making peg dolls, baking wheaten scones and flying kites.

Open: Monday–Saturday, 1000–1700; Sunday, 1400–1700

EXTRA . . . EXTRA . . . As you enter Haggs Castle, take a look at the inscription above the door. It notes this as the residence of John Maxwell – way back in 1585.

HUNTERIAN ART GALLERY, University of Glasgow, 82 Hillhead Street. Tel: 041-330 5431

The Hunterian Art Gallery is a gem not to be missed. The nucleus of the collection is the bequest of William Hunter (1718–83) which includes 17th-century Dutch and Flemish masters. However, Hunter's collection has been extended, most notably with the Whistler collection and the Mackintosh House and collection. The works on display by James Abbott McNeill Whistler (1834–1903) are rivalled only by those in the Freer Gallery in Washington. You can see some of his most atmospheric works, like his Thames night-pieces which he called 'Nocturns', alongside his more stylized designs, like 'Cartoon for the Peacock Room', which show his clear fascination with Far Eastern art. The reconstructed home of Charles Rennie Mackintosh (*see page 52*) offers a real contrast. The four main rooms of this important architect's house in Southpark Avenue have been carefully reconstructed and filled with his own furniture. The result, even if not to your taste, is undeniably stunning. And, as you walk over the pale-coloured carpet around the architects' furnishings and fittings, you can't help but understand something of the special qualities of this outstanding designer. (*See also walk 3*)

Open: Monday–Friday, 0930–1700; Saturday, 0930–1300
　　　　(Mackintosh House: free weekday mornings only)

EXTRA . . . EXTRA . . . To enter the Hunterian Art
Gallery you must push open an impressive pair of alumin-
ium doors which are works of art in their own right.
Commissioned from Scotland's most famous living sculp-
tor, Eduardo Paolozzi, they're a fittingly triumphal
entrance to the treasures of the gallery.

HUNTERIAN MUSEUM, University of Glasgow, University Avenue. Tel: 041-330 4221

Opened in 1807, this was Scotland's first public museum.
In it you'll find a major display showing the achievements
of the university and all sorts of exhibits from William
Hunter's collection (*see Hunterian Art Gallery, page 77*)
There are geological displays illustrating the changing
Scottish landscape over some 3,000 million years. The
archaeological section has displays which depict early
Egypt as well as telling Scotland's story from the end of
the Ice Age. But it's the world-famous Hunter coin
cabinet which attracts experts from around the globe. It
includes silver coins from the period of Julius Ceasar. (*See
also walk 3*)

Open: Monday–Friday, 0930–1700; Saturday, 0930–1300

EXTRA . . . EXTRA . . . Before formal naming sys-
tems were developed, fossilized fish were given women's
names. Look out for 'Ann'; 2 inches (5cm) long 'she' is

330 million years old and was found in the carboniferous rocks at Bearsden.

KELVINGROVE ART GALLERY AND MUSEUM, Argyle Street. Tel: 041-357 3929

You'd do well to make a careful study of the museum plan (in the entrance foyer) before you begin to look at the collection because, as you'll quickly realize as you pass through into the cavernous entrance hall, Kelvingrove Museum and Art Gallery is huge! Don't attempt to take in more than a small section on one visit – it's just too daunting. Instead, plan to come back for a second helping. There's a large section devoted to archaeology – its main theme is Scottish prehistory, but there are Egyptian and Cypriot displays too. In the nearby ethnography gallery you can see items from the South Pacific, Japan and North America – just a small part of an extensive collection which illustrates cultures of other continents. Natural history is also well represented with a comprehensive collection of British birds as well as sections on zoology, geology and botany. In the fine art gallery you can see works from all the major European schools: the examples of the Dutch 17th century, the French Barbizon group, the Impressionists and the Post Impressionists are particularly stunning. And the decorative arts haven't been forgotten either; look out for ceramics, glass, silver, jewellery and furniture; they come from right across Western Europe. (*See also walk 3*)

Open: Monday–Saturday, 1000–1700; Sunday, 1400–1700

EXTRA . . . EXTRA . . . The gallery and museum are housed in an imposing red-sandstone building. It is the work of John W. Simpson and E. J. Milner Allen and was first opened to the public in 1902.

LOCHWINNOCH MUSEUM, High Street, Lochwinnoch (off A760).
Tel: Lochwinnoch 842615

Lochwinnoch Museum is a tiny, purpose-built extension to the village library (which is housed in the old village school house) and it is best to see it in combination with a visit to nearby Castle Semple Country Park (*see page 103*). The museum, which opened in 1984, changes its exhibitions regularly, but the displays are always drawn from the Renfrew district's own collections. The exhibitions might, for example, reflect the area's predominantly rural way of life or might show one of its many crafts like silk weaving or furniture making. (*See also Renfrew, page 157*)

Open: Monday, Wednesday, Friday, 1000–1300, 1400–1700 and 1800–2000; Tuesday and Saturday, 1000–1300 and 1400–1700

EXTRA . . . EXTRA . . . Just behind the museum's entrance door you'll find an enlarged black and white photograph of the employees of Joseph Johnstone Ltd (a furniture manufacturer during the 1930s). It has proved to be the most popular exhibit as many of the people in it are either still alive or are recognized by relatives. But there are still some unknown faces – if you recognize someone, the curator would like to hear from you.

McLEAN MUSEUM AND ART GALLERY, 9 Union Street, Greenock. Tel: Greenock 23741

If you arrive at the McLean Museum and Art Gallery expecting a small museum of local interest, you'll be in for a surprise. True, the building is relatively small, but the collection contains many real works of art. It spans a variety of fields of interest – craft, painting, ceramics, armoury, models, fossils, science and industry. Indeed, only a small proportion of the collection can be displayed at any one time. You might see the painting 'Bordeaux' by Boudin, or perhaps Corbet's 'Women with Sticks'. There are some delightful Japanese Netsuke and an exquisite 19th-century Chinese ship which has been modelled in ivory. A fragment of an Egyptian temple can be studied here along with a pair of 19th-century bead-work moccasins originating from the Canadian Great Lakes. So, take a chance; this is one time when you're almost certain to be lucky!

Note: the museum may close sections to put up new displays and for renovation

Open: Monday–Saturday, 1000–1200 and 1300–1700

EXTRA . . . EXTRA . . . While you're in the town of Greenock, why not take the opportunity to explore its architectural heritage? A few buildings to look out for are listed below.

Customhouse, Customhouse Quay
The customhouse was built in 1818 by William Burn and it is still one of the most outstanding pieces of architecture on Clydeside.

The Dutch Gable, William Street
Greenock's oldest building, the Dutch Gable dates from 1755.

Watt Library, Union Street
The McLean Museum building is tucked away behind the impressive façade of the Watt Library. It was built in 1837 in northern English Tudor style.

MUSEUM OF THE 602 (CITY OF GLASGOW) SQUADRON, Queen Elizabeth Avenue, Hillington. Tel: 041-882 6201 Ext. 105

If you're interested in the RAF, do pay a visit to 602 Squadron museum. You'll be fascinated by this evocative tribute to a famous squadron. A visit takes the form of a tour lead by a true enthusiast – so be prepared for an hour or so discussing the many pieces of memorabilia and old photographs on display; each picture tells a story and every item belonged to someone of note. Look out for the Battle of Britain tie and the book containing the names of men who took part in this famous battle – it is kept open on the page which shows the signatures of the survivors.

Open: Wednesday and Friday, 1930–2130 (closed July and August)

EXTRA . . . EXTRA . . . 602 was the only squadron allowed to wear the tartan kilt as part of mess dress!

PAISLEY MUSEUM AND ART GALLERY, High Street, Paisley. Tel: 041-889 3151

This is an excellent local museum which has a good natural-history section, an interesting selection of 20th-century ceramic work, and some beautiful paintings. However, its most important display is, without doubt, its collection of Paisley shawls. Weaving is a centuries-old tradition in Paisley, but it was the distinctive teardrop pattern which really put the skills of the community on the map at the beginning of the 19th century. In fact, the pattern doesn't originate from Paisley, but can be traced to Indo-European cultures dating back some 2,000 years. Shawls were imported from Kashmir by the East India Company but were prohibitively expensive. Paisley weavers worked hard to supply the demand and succeeded in establishing the fashionable design as their own with the term 'Paisley' becoming known throughout the world. (*See also Renfrew, page 157*)

Open: Monday–Saturday, 1000–1700

EXTRA . . . EXTRA . . . Make a slight detour into nearby New Street and you'll be treated to another outstanding example of design, this time Art Nouveau. The Bull Inn dates from 1901 and it retains much of its original decorative interior fittings as well as an impressive façade.

THE PEOPLE'S PALACE, Glasgow Green.
Tel: 041-554 0223

If you're a newcomer to Glasgow, the People's Palace is a great introduction to the history of the city and its people. If you've already discovered this fascinating museum, then you'll probably want to go again and again – it's the kind of place where you always seem to discover something new! The exhibits are on three floors and tell the story of Glasgow from its foundation in 1175 to the present day through the eyes of the people who lived and worked here. Every corner is filled with beautifully presented collections relating to trades and industries, religion, labour movements, entertainment, sport, arts and crafts, and famous personalities through the ages – from St Mungo to Billy Connolly! Set in the heart of Glasgow Green (*see page 112*), the museum was opened in 1898 as a cultural centre for the East End of Glasgow and over the years has built up such a high reputation it attracts visitors from near and far. Adjoining are the Winter Gardens, a treasure-house of shrubs and flowers, which also serve as a tea room and showcase for some unusual exhibits – including a parish church bell of 1862.

Open: Monday–Saturday, 1000–1700; Sunday, 1400–1700

EXTRA . . . EXTRA . . . The Winter Gardens are modelled on the inverted hull of Lord Nelson's flagship *Victory*, a tribute to the fact they're so close to the first monument in Britain erected to commemorate Nelson.

POLLOK HOUSE, 2060 Pollokshaws Road.
Tel: 041-632 0274

Pollok House, in the glorious setting of Pollok Country Park (*see page 121*) was the ancestral home of the Maxwell family. The central part of the house, which is thought to have been the work of the renowned architects William and John Adam, dates from c. 1750. Undoubtedly Glasgow's most impressive and important surviving piece of 18th-century domestic architecture, Pollok House is also home for one of the finest collections of Spanish paintings in Britain. Here you'll find works by El Greco, Murillo and Goya. The furnishings are interesting too – look out for the intricate astronomical clock which has been associated with Pollok House for generations. And do remember to look out of the windows; the views are particularly beautiful from the library which looks out on to a formal garden. (*See also walk 4*)

Open: Monday–Saturday, 1000–1700; Sunday, 1400–1700

EXTRA . . . EXTRA . . . Make sure you see the remarkable model of Cruckston Castle; it's a memorial to the Cruckston Yew from which it is made. The wood has been cut into square pieces, about an 8th of an inch (3.5mm) in size, to resemble stones. Then, with great precision, the model was quite literally built – stone by stone.

PRIVATE GALLERIES

There are several private art galleries in the city, particularly in the Bath Street area, which hold permanent and changing exhibitions. The idea is obviously to sell the works of art but everyone is welcome to browse. For a full list contact the Greater Glasgow Tourist Board, 35–39 St Vincent Place, Glasgow G1 2ER. Tel: 041-227 4885. Here are just a few of those worth visiting.

Annan Gallery, 130 West Campbell Street.
Tel: 041-221 5087
Although the walls are lined with some very fine original paintings by Scottish and continental artists, this gallery is best known for its amazing collection of 500 or so old 12-inch (30.5cm) glass plate negatives of Glasgow dating back to the mid-19th century. Show some interest and you'll be treated to a private viewing of these fascinating photographs.

Open: Monday–Friday, 0900–1700; Saturday, 0930–1230

Cyril Gerber Gallery, 148 West Regent Street.
Tel: 041-221 3095
Opened by Cyril Gerber, founder of the Compass Gallery (*see page 74*), this basement gallery is a pleasant place to enjoy contemporary works of art. Most of its hanging space is devoted to work by Scottish artists, in particular the Glasgow School, both past and present. Three or four special exhibitions are held every year.

Open: Monday–Friday, 0930–1730; Saturday, 0930–1230

Metro Gallery, 713 Great Western Road.
Tel: 041-339 0737

A little further out of the centre, this gallery, which is conveniently placed for the Botanic Gardens (*see page 100*), specializes in limited-edition prints and water-colours by Scottish artists. They have a reputation for excellent temporary exhibitions.

Open: Tuesday–Saturday, 1030–1700

EXTRA . . . EXTRA . . . A week-long art exhibition with a very local flavour is held every October in the Town Hall at Kirkintilloch. Everyone is welcome to show their work, and exhibits include pottery, paintings, framed embroideries and much more. For further details (and perhaps an entry form) contact: Strathkelvin District Council, Library HQ, 170 Kirkintilloch Road, Bishopbriggs, Glasgow G84 2LX. Tel: 041-762 0112.

PROVAND'S LORDSHIP, 3 Castle Street.
Tel: 041-552 8819

Provand's Lordship, one of the few surviving mediaeval buildings to be found in Glasgow, dates from 1471. Standing opposite the imposing bulk of Glasgow Cathedral (*see page 45*) and the fascinating necropolis (*see page 56*), it completes an atmospheric triangle which should not be missed on a visit to the city. It's thought that the house was once the residence of the Preceptor (master) of a group of almshouses which belonged to the long-since-vanished St Nicholas Hospital. Later the building became a manse for one of the cathedral's canons. When much of the church's lands were secularized during the Reformation, the canon of the time, one William Baillie, obtained from Queen Mary a charter allowing him to become a lay laird. Legend has it that Mary stayed in Provand's Lordship in January 1567 while visiting the ailing Darnley. Today the oldest house in Glasgow has been turned into a popular museum with displays dating from 1500 to 1914 including a collection of 17th-century furniture.

Open: Monday–Saturday, 1000–1700; Sunday, 1400–1700

EXTRA . . . EXTRA . . . In all, Glasgow Cathedral was surrounded by some 32 manses and most of the clergy who lived in them had their prebend or living outside the city boundary. Indeed, the canon who lived in this sole surviving manse held a prebend in Lanarkshire; prebend lands became known as 'provan' or 'provand' – hence the title, 'Provand's Lordship'.

ROYAL HIGHLAND FUSILIERS MUSEUM,
518 Sauchiehall Street. Tel: 041-332 0961

Three hundred years of the infantry of Glasgow and Ayrshire are on display in this small, well laid out museum. It is packed with memorabilia including medals, swords, silverware, statues and uniforms. The Royal Highland Fusiliers took its present title in 1959 when the Royal Scots Fusiliers and the Highland Light Infantry were amalgamated. The regiment is unique in that it carries three colours and has been awarded the greatest number of battle honours of any regiment. (*See also walk* 7)

Open: Monday–Thursday, 0900–1630; Friday, 0900–1600

EXTRA . . . EXTRA . . . If you want a bit of fun, try and discover why three colours are carried by the regiment; when a British king last commanded his army in the field; and who got a 'wee dram' for doing a big job!

RUTHERGLEN MUSEUM OF LOCAL HISTORY, King Street, Rutherglen (off A730)

Now a suburb of Glasgow, Rutherglen has a surprisingly long and distinguished history. Indeed, it was one of the nine or ten towns to be created a royal burgh by David I during his reign, 1124–53, and has many legendary tales attached to its name. The museum traces the town's past through changing displays and exhibitions of artefacts, pictures, photographs and archaeological finds. An item of special interest is the binnacle of the *Lucy Ashton*, a famous Clyde steamer built in the town's old shipyard, but you'll find all the exhibits help shed light on little-known aspects of the town's history. After a visit, you'll feel inspired to explore Rutherglen for yourself.

Open: Monday–Saturday, 1000–1700; Sunday, 1400–1700

EXTRA . . . EXTRA . . . The low steeple in Main Street is all that remains of the parish church. It was here, in 1297, the story goes, that a truce between England and Scotland was made and Sir John Menteith agreed to betray William Wallace.

SCOTLAND STREET SCHOOL MUSEUM OF EDUCATION, 225 Scotland Street.
Tel: 041-429 1202

Scotland Street School was designed by Charles Rennie Mackintosh (*see page 52*) and opened in 1906. First an infant school, then a primary school, it today provides an ideal setting for a museum of education. School groups are shown how pupils were taught at the turn of the century. Dressed in period costume they get the chance to sit on old school benches and learn 'sums' from a teacher who writes on the blackboard. But for adults a tour tends to be a more nostalgic affair as black-and-white photographs, inkwells and a headmaster's desk bring back old memories.

Open: Monday–Thursday, 1000–1200, 1400–1600; Friday, 1000–1200, 1400–1530

EXTRA . . . EXTRA . . . The museum collects educational memorabilia – if you've something you'd like to donate, they'd love to hear from you.

SCOTTISH DESIGN CENTRE, 72 St Vincent Street. Tel: 041-221 6121

Light, bright and airy, the Scottish Design Centre is quite simply a very pleasant place to be. There's a shop selling interesting goodies, a cafeteria serving appetizing treats and the 'for free' part of it all: a series of changing exhibitions which act as a showcase for some of the best of British-manufactured consumer goods. The standard of design is high, the displays usually imaginative and exciting and the types of goods exhibited amazingly varied ranging from high-tech developments in musical instruments to the work of the charity, Intermediate Technology Development Group, and the technologies, tools and equipment it is using to help in developing countries. You can never be quite sure what you'll find, but one thing's for certain – you won't be disappointed! (*See also walk 7*)

Open: Monday–Friday, 0930–1700; Saturday, 0900–1700

EXTRA . . . EXTRA . . . Further along St Vincent Street at Nos. 142–4 is a building known as the Hatrack – for obvious reasons! Designed in 1899 by James Salmon, an architect nicknamed 'Wee Trout' because of his size, it's anything but wee – ten storeys high and very narrow, you can't help but look up and up!

SPRINGBURN MUSEUM AND EXHIBITION CENTRE, Springburn Library, Ayr Street. Tel: 041-558 5559

The great thing about this small but enterprizing museum, run by volunteer staff and relying almost entirely on local donations, is that it is expanding in content and interest all the time. The exhibits, which are largely pictorial, cover the social history of the area highlighting its link with the railways. However, it is very much a museum that moves with the times and a record is kept of all the changes in Springburn with displays showing buildings which have been recently demolished or events that have involved the community. Changing exhibitions are held regularly with topics ranging from Radical Glasgow to the

Cowlairs works with models of locomotives, union badges and old tools.

Open: All year, Monday–Friday, 1030–1700; Saturday, 1000–1300; Sunday, 1400–1700

EXTRA . . . EXTRA . . . The museum adjoins the local library which has an excellent selection of books on the history of the area. There's a comfortable sitting space where you're free to browse through them at your leisure.

SUMMERLEE HERITAGE MUSEUM, West Canal Street, Coatbridge (M8, Exit 10). Tel: Coatbridge 31261

A museum devoted to Scotland's industrial heritage couldn't be better positioned than here at Coatbridge (*see Monklands, page 156*). The museum has been built around the extensive remains of Summerlee Iron-works, an early hot-blast ironworks which opened in 1837. From various viewpoints on the museum's site you can see the flues, ducts, pipes and distinctive circular bases of the blast furnaces. But the most noticeable aspect of a visit to Summerlee is the noise. This is a reconstructed *working* environment and at times it can be quite deafening and even smelly! Inside the visually striking machine-exhibition hall, which covers some 132,000 square yards you can see forges, a foundry, a tinsmith and blacksmith along with a comprehensive collection of engineering tools and equipment. There are whirring belts, slides, gears and pulleys all recalling a time when the engineering skills of this area sustained shipbuilding and iron making.

Open: Easter–end September, daily, 1000–1700

EXTRA . . . EXTRA . . . Summerlee Ironworks was built on the banks of the Monklands canal. The canal linked the rich Monklands coalfield with Glasgow and the Clyde. It was engineered by James Watt.

THIRD EYE CENTRE, 350 Sauchiehall Street. Tel: 041-332 7521/4

The Third Eye Centre is considered, by many, to be Scotland's leading arts centre – some 250,000 people visit its bookshop, studio theatre, exhibitions and coffee shop each year. The *Glasgow Herald* described it as 'a cultural powerhouse'; well, you'll have to decide for yourself whether it's to your taste. Exhibitions, which are held in its two galleries, cafe and foyer area, are of contemporary work by Scottish, UK and international artists and include photography, popular culture and Glasgow issues. (*See also Poetry Readings, page 33, Lectures, page 28 and walk 1*)

Open: Tuesday–Saturday, 1000–1730; Sunday, 1400–1730

EXTRA . . . EXTRA . . . This is *the* place to pick up leaflets about the many arts events happening in the city.

THE THOMAS MUIR MUSEUM, Huntershill House Crowhill Road, Bishopbriggs (off A803). Tel: 041-772 8592

Thomas Muir (1765–99), the radical thinker who became so involved in electoral reform in the 1790s, lived at nearby Huntershill, Bishopbriggs, and this collection is devoted to his life and achievements. Exhibits and displays highlight his efforts to set up reform societies, his arrest and transportation to Botany Bay, his escape and dangerous journeys around the world, and finally his death in Paris in 1799, aged only 33. It's a moving tribute giving a new insight into one of the little-recognized fathers of modern democracy. (*See also Strathkelvin, page 158*)

Open: by request to the curator

EXTRA . . . EXTRA . . . Muir was an elder at nearby Cadder parish church. The parish dates back to the 12th century and the present church (open to visitors) was built around 1830.

TRANSPORT MUSEUM, Kelvin Hall, Bunhouse Road. Tel: 041-357 3929

As Glasgow flourished during Victorian times – an age which saw huge steps forward in modes of transport – it isn't surprising to find an exciting transport museum in the heart of the city. The history of transport is shown through a wide range of vehicles: you can see gleaming, red fire engines and a steam-powered traction engine; there's a road roller and perhaps the oldest surviving pedal cycle in the world. The car collection includes classics such as the Ford Model T, a Rolls-Royce, a Bentley and Jackie Stewart's world-beating Tyrrell Ford. Look out for the trams or, as they were once called, Glaswegian love 'caurs'! And don't miss the shipping collection, it is ranked as outstanding in world terms. The collection boasts some 600 models – many of them builders' models – and traces the development of shipbuilding on the Clyde. (*See also walk 3*)

Open: Monday–Saturday, 1000–1700; Sunday, 1400–1700

EXTRA . . . EXTRA . . . Kelvin Hall, now developed into the Transport Museum and a sports complex, was once the venue for major concerts and exhibitions including motor shows and circuses – you name it, it's probably been on show here!

ZOOLOGY MUSEUM, Department of Zoology, Glasgow University, University Avenue. Tel: 041-339 8855 Ext. 5506

This is the Zoological collection of the Hunterian Museum (*see page 78*) but it has been displayed separately, here in the university zoological department, since 1923. Specimens on display are regularly used for teaching purposes and in particular to show how animals are classified. The museum concentrates on extant species of animals, but fascinating exhibits do include many strange items which can no longer be found on earth. Take, for instance, the egg of the giant Elephant Bird of Madagascar – the largest egg ever produced by a bird – which became extinct in the 13th century.

Open: weekdays, by appointment only

EXTRA . . . EXTRA . . . Beside the zoology department building stands the West Medical Building which is the work of architect James Miller. Its early Renaissance motifs create stylistic links with the main university building which is by Gilbert Scott.

CHAPTER FOUR
Parks and Open Spaces

AUCHINLEA PARK, Auchinlea Road.

Just a stone's throw from the busy M8, this park is relatively undiscovered compared to Glasgow's other parks. There has been a concentrated effort at maintenance in recent years and the park has been redesigned and replanted to show parkland of three different and very distinct types: firstly the formal garden designed as an old knot garden, then the more natural garden where award-winning shrubs are on display, and finally the wilder areas with marshland plants flourishing in the bog gardens. With more plans for future projects, it is a park worth remembering.

Open: daily, dawn to dusk

EXTRA . . . EXTRA . . . Provan Hall stands at the Auchinlea Road entrance to the park. This 15th-century building is believed to be one of the few pre-Reformation domestic buildings left in Scotland. It is now a community centre.

BELLAHOUSTON PARK, Mosspark Boulevard/Paisley Road West.

Relatively large, yet simply laid out, Bellahouston Park attracts sports enthusiasts from the surrounding area. It contains a multi-purpose indoor sports centre as well as an all-weather arena with a seven-lane running track. At the turn of the century some 12 acres of nursery were established here to provide the Parks Department with trees and shrubs. But its heyday was 1938 – the year of the Empire Exhibition. Make for the statue of George VI, which commemorates the exhibition, and you'll have a good view over Glasgow.

Open: daily, dawn to dusk

EXTRA . . . EXTRA . . . If you look on a map you'll see that there's a building in the park named Palace of Art – it's the only remaining building from the Empire Exhibition. But don't be tempted to seek it out; today it is used as an educational centre!

BOTANIC GARDENS, Great Western Road

Give yourself plenty of time to enjoy the Botanic Gardens – the hours just seem to disappear as you become pleasantly absorbed in the beauty around you. It's a place to sit and ponder, stand and stare, and marvel at the world of nature: the huge banana tree that bears fruit, the hanging tropical gourds, the sensitive plants whose leaves close up and drop down at the slightest touch, rare and exotic orchids and the fleshy succulent plants . . .

Perhaps one of the best places to start is at Kibble Palace near the entrance on Queen Margaret Drive. This 23,000 square foot (2090 square m) Victorian glasshouse, considered to be one of the finest buildings in the city, originally belonged to an eccentric engineer, John Kibble, who used it as a conservatory for his private house. In 1873 he decided to transfer it to the Botanic Gardens and brought it up the Clyde on a raft drawn by a 'puffer'! Known then as 'Kibble Crystal Art Palace', it was used as a concert hall and meeting place – Gladstone and Disraeli both gave their rectorial addresses here. Today, Kibble Palace is a winter garden and home to an outstanding collection of tree ferns, mostly from New Zealand and Australia. Circling the ferns are Victorian Camellias set amidst marble statues, and a geographical display of plants from temperate regions. The palace also houses the visitors' centre, a permanent exhibition on the history of the plant kingdom, and changing topical displays. Outside are the herb garden, rock garden and systematic garden – all neatly labelled, with plants arranged in botanical families or according to their uses – with paths leading through 42 acres of ever-changing hues to what for many people is the highlight of a visit: the main range of glasshouses. As you step inside you're greeted by the bright colours of the flowers in the conservatory. This is the start of a tour of plants and shrubs growing in their natural environments, a collection that seems to cover almost every corner of the world.

The gardens were founded in 1817 when Thomas Hopkirk donated his own collection of plants to the Royal Botanic Institution of Glasgow for the research and study of botany and medicine. They soon gained a world-wide reputation and moved to their present site in 1842, where they were opened to the public on Saturdays for one shilling (five new pence) and on occasions were 'thrown open to the Working Classes on the payment of one penny each'. The gardens still combine their original purpose of providing material for serious botanical research with pleasure for everyone – but these days, there's no charge at all!

Open: Gardens, 0700-dusk; Kibble Palace, 1000-1645
　　　　(summer), 1000–1615 (winter); Main Range,
　　　　Monday–Saturday, 1300–1645 (summer),
　　　　1300–1615 (winter); Sundays, 1200–1645
　　　　(summer), 1200–1615 (winter)

EXTRA . . . EXTRA . . . By all accounts John Kibble,
who built Kibble Palace, was a strange character – among
his more dubious claims to fame are that he cycled across
Loch Long on a bicycle fitted with floats and took the
largest photographs of the 19th century from inside a
camera drawn by a horse and cart!

CAMPSIE FELLS (off A891)

A hill walker's paradise, that's the Campsie Fells! This
area of volcanic moorland which stretches from Lennox-
town in the south to Fintry in the north rises to over 1800
feet (550 m) and offers some really amazing views over
the Clyde valley and beyond. A good starting point for
walks is the picturesque village of Milton of Campsie
where footpaths, well-trodden by villagers and visitors
over the years take you over the lower parts of the fells
and then lead you into the wilder, more unexplored areas.
It's a stretch of changing scenery, particularly beautiful in
the springtime when lambs frolic among the daffodils,
wood pigeons call from the trees and if you're lucky you
can see roe deer roaming the hills. For suggested walks
through the Campsie Fells, booklets are available (at a
nominal charge) from Bishopbriggs Library, 170 Kirkintilloch Road, Bishopbriggs. Tel: 041-772 4513. (*See also
Strathkelvin, page 158*)

Open: all the time

EXTRA ... EXTRA ... The Campsie Fells are crossed by Crow Road. According to legend it was along this road that St Mungo and his bulls pulled the body of the holy man, Fergus, until they reached a cemetery where St Mungo buried him. It was at the burial spot that he founded a church, a forerunner of the present day Glasgow Cathedral. (*See page 45 and also Glasgow's Coat of Arms, page 11*)

CASTLE SEMPLE COUNTRY PARK (off A760). Tel: Lochwinnoch 842882

Many people come to Castle Semple Country Park to fish (there's plenty of pike and perch in the water) or to take part in water activities like canoeing and sailing (there is a launching charge). However, there's plenty for nature lovers and walkers. Parkhill wood, once part of Castle Semple estate grounds, is a particularly lovely area to explore. There's a spectacular rhododendron maze known locally as '50 passages' (best seen in May when the rhododendrons are in full bloom), grottoes, ice houses, follies and fish ponds including some ancient ones which were once stocked with trout to feed the monks of Paisley Abbey (*see page 58*). If you're a keen bird spotter, look out for whooper, greylag geese, widgeon and goldeneye during the winter, and snipe, reed bunting, coot, water rail and tufted duck all the year round. To discover more about the country park, start your visit at the information centre. Here you'll find a useful 3-D model of the area which shows the extent of the loch and its surrounding countryside including parts which have been designated areas of special scientific interest (no public access). The ranger on duty will be able to point the way to the attractions mentioned above. (*See also Renfrew, page 157*)

Open: park: all the time; information centre: daily mid-October to start of British summer time, 0900–1630; summer, 0830–dusk

---

EXTRA . . . EXTRA . . . Take a look at Collegiate Church at Low Semple. Roofless, it is nevertheless important enough to have been listed as an ancient building.

CATHKIN BRAES PARK, Cathkin Road, High Burnside

Choose a clear day for your visit to Cathkin Braes Park and you can enjoy a quite spectacular view from the highest point, Queen Mary's Seat. You're around 600 feet (180 m) above sea level here and to the east you can see Arthur's Seat in Edinburgh and the Pentland Hills; to the west the Braes of Gleniffer and Fereneze and in the distance, Goatfell. To the north, Ben Lomond rises high, and Ben Ledi and the Cobbler . . . To help you find your way around, a viewpoint plaque identifies the different peaks. The park covers around 72 acres and is really quite wild – but that's just the way Mr James Dick, the man who presented it to the city in 1886, wanted it to be. His wish was that it 'remains as nearly as possible an expanse of primitive hillside, with its crags and knolls, its natural grass, and its haphazard clumps of trees, brushwood, bushes, untouched by the formal hand of the landscape gardener', so don't expect any neat floral displays, rose gardens or bowling greens! There aren't any picnic tables either, but if you're prepared to rough it a bit you'll find Cathkin Braes Park one of the most picturesque spots in Glasgow for a picnic.

Open: all the time

EXTRA . . . EXTRA . . . To the west of the park is the Big Wood, another exciting place for a walk.

CUSTOM HOUSE QUAY GARDENS, Clyde Street

This stretch of disused quayside has now been transformed into a lovely walkway on the north side of the River Clyde (*see page 125*). The gardens, which are on different levels, run from Glasgow Bridge (*see page 45*) to Victoria Bridge and although they're so near the city centre they are a delightful place to walk or sit especially during the summer when buskers provide background music. Moored alongside Victoria Bridge and making a point of interest on the walkway is the old clipper ship *SV Carrick*. Formerly known as the *City of Adelaide* it was built in 1864, a contemporary of the *Cutty Sark*. It is now the headquarters of the Royal Naval Volunteer Reserve Club and although you can't go inside, it is impressive from the outside. (*See also walk 2*)

Open: all the time

EXTRA . . . EXTRA . . . Custom House itself is at the Glasgow Bridge end of Clyde Street. Opened in 1840, it was designed by John Taylor who also designed the Custom House at Dundee. Far from being an eminent Scottish architect of the day, he was an Irish-born Customs official!

DAWSHOLM PARK, Islay Road

Wooded and wonderful, with the River Kelvin making its peaceful way through the middle, Dawsholm Park, all 72 acres of it, has been left largely in its natural state and is a real treat for nature lovers. It is particularly beautiful in the autumn when the fallen leaves cover the footpaths, a carpet in shades of gold and bronze, but whatever time of year you visit, you'll find animals scampering in the undergrowth, squirrels climbing the trees, birds singing cheerfully and a whole host of wild plants – you'll need to take a nature book to identify everything! And do make sure you enjoy the views – look northwards to Perthshire and Argyll, and southwards to Ayrshire and Lanarkshire.

Open: all the time

EXTRA . . . EXTRA . . . If you choose a clear day and stand on the highest point in the park, you can see eight counties before you.

DRUMPELLIER COUNTRY PARK,
Coatbridge. Tel: Ranger: Coatbridge 22574; General enquiries: Coatbridge 22257

Start your visit at the award-winning visitor centre and you'll be able to discover some of the many things to do and see in Drumpellier. It is situated in a beautiful spot beside Lochend Loch and looks out over the water to the wooded area of the park beyond. Two trails have been devised to help you find your way through the park. Things to look out for along the routes include oaks, Corsican pines and Norwegian maples; great crested grebes and reed buntings; trout, eel and pike; Japanese knotweed, yellow iris, marsh marigold and dog violets; roe deer, foxes, weasels and water vole. There's also a whole host of butterflies to spot: garden tiger, meadow brown, small tortoiseshell. And so the list could go on. This is definitely a park for people who want to enjoy nature and the rangers are very willing to point you in the right direction.

Note: a visit here links well with a visit to Summerlee Heritage Museum (*see page 92*) – it is certainly quite a contrast! Ask at either for details of a canal walkway. (*See also Monklands, page 156*)

Open: daily until dusk

EXTRA . . . EXTRA . . . Lochend Loch was lived on by ancient people. Some 500 tons of stone, earth and timber was dumped into the water to form a muddy mound – an artificially constructed island known as a crannog. You can see a reconstruction beside the original site which is thought to have burned down twice.

FORTH AND CLYDE CANAL, Kelvin
Aqueduct to Spiers Wharf

Thanks to the efforts of volunteers and enthusiasts, you can now walk along this 3½-mile (5.3km) stretch of towpath from Kelvin Aqueduct (*see also Kelvin Walkway, page 114*) to Spiers Wharf. It is a walk rich in industrial heritage (look out for the historic Maryhill Lock), natural beauty and a whole variety of things to see and do. You'll pass rare and beautiful plants, hear wildlife scampering in the undergrowth and come across lock-keepers' cottages, old swing and lifting bridges and canalside stables – in fact, if there's one piece of advice it is to take a camera!

There's lots of canal traffic to enjoy too – most notably the old Clyde passenger ferry *Ferry Queen* which sails from Glasgow Road Bridge and the specially equipped *Yarrow Seagull*, run by the Seagull Trust, giving disabled children a chance to cruise on the canal for free. Then there's all the sporting activities – the canal is a popular spot for fishing and the towpath acts as a good training route for cyclists, runners and joggers. By the time you arrive at Spiers Wharf you'll probably be feeling completely exhausted by all the activity along the way, but if you have any energy left, cross Craighill Road, take the first turn on your left, and you can continue following the canal to Port Dundas.

For a free leaflet on the canal and any further information contact: Forth and Clyde Canal Project Officer, British Waterways Leisure, Canal House, Applecross Street, Glasgow G4 9SP. Tel: 041-332 6936. For details of events, activities and ways in which you can help with the restoration and upkeep of the canal contact: Forth and Clyde Canal Society, 32 Clouston Street, Glasgow G20 8QU (enclose sae).

Open: all the time

EXTRA . . . EXTRA . . . The Forth and Clyde Canal was cut between Grangemouth and Bowling between 1768 and 1790. The Glasgow branch was added in 1793 joining it up with the Monklands Canal. It was 35 miles (76km) long rising to a summit above sea level of 158 feet (47m), with a total of 39 locks. The canal was closed to navigation in 1963.

GEORGE SQUARE

If you're visiting Glasgow for the first time, George Square is a good place for you to begin to explore the city. From here you can easily walk to many of the city's main attractions (*see walk 1*). A focal point for Glasgow's business activities, it is a bustling square with congested traffic moving slowly on all four sides. However, the open space itself *is* something of a haven with colourfully planted flower beds and a plentiful supply of benches. So why not take a seat and have a look around you? You should be able to spot the Bank of Scotland, the Merchants' House, the Post Office and, along the whole length of the eastern side, the imposing Renaissance-style frontage of the City Chambers (*see page 42*). There are lots of statues too:

Prince Albert Queen Victoria's consort (they married in 1840) sits sedately on his horse in this work by Marochetti, erected in 1866.

Robert Burns In this statue, by George Ewing, erected in 1877 Robert Burns (1759–96), the most famous of all Scottish poets (his works include 'Tam o'Shanter', 'To a Haggis', 'The Banks o'Doon'), stands almost regally and surveys all that's before him.

Thomas Campbell Born in nearby High Street, Thomas Campbell was Lord Rector of Glasgow University (1826–8). This statue by Mossman was erected in 1877.

Lord Clyde A soldier in the Crimean War, Lord Clyde is remembered as the man who crushed the Indian Mutiny of 1858. He died in 1863 and this statue by Foley was erected in 1868.

William E. Gladstone Gladstone (1809–98) received the Freedom of the City of Glasgow in 1865 at which time he held the office of Prime Minister. This statue, which is the work of Thornycroft, was erected in 1902.

Dr Thomas Graham This statue by Broadie shows Dr Thomas Graham (1805–69) in a thoughtful mood, as befits a lecturer in chemistry at Anderson's College and Master of the Mint.

Sir John Moore Sir John Moore was born in Trongate (*see page 49*) in 1761; the hero of Corunna, he was killed in battle in 1809. This statue by Flaxman was erected in 1819 – making it the first statue in the square.

James Oswald Member of Parliament for Glasgow (1832–7), James Oswald (1779–1852) played an important role in the passing of the Parliamentary Reform Bill of 1832. His statue by Marochetti was erected in 1875.

Sir Robert Peel This statue by Mossman, which depicts Sir Robert Peel (1788–1850), the Prime Minister known for the repeal of the Corn Laws, was erected in 1859.

Sir Walter Scott *The Lady of the Lake*, *Rob Roy*, *The Waverley Novels*. Novelist Sir Walter Scott (1771–1832) has quite a number of well-known titles to his name. This statue by Greenshields, erected in 1837, was the first of many memorials to this great writer. It is certainly prominent standing on an 80ft column!

Queen Victoria In a city which thrived during Victorian times, it isn't surprising to find a majestic statue of Queen Victoria, who reigned from 1837 to 1901. This one by Marochetti was placed in George Square in 1865.

James Watt James Watt (1736–1819), instrument maker and civil engineer, designed the first viable steam engine which was patented in 1796 (*see Glasgow Green page 112*). Erected in 1832, this statue is by Chantry.

The Cenotaph Most important of all the memorials in George Square is the Cenotaph by Sir John Burnet. Unveiled in 1924 by Field Marshal Earl Haig, it bears the inscription 'Their Name liveth evermore'.
Note: as many of the buildings around George Square are floodlit it is a good place to visit after dark.

Open: all the time

EXTRA . . . EXTRA . . . The square was named in honour of George III. That's surprising because it was George III who, by losing the American colonies, destroyed Glasgow's flourishing tobacco trade. 'Tobacco Lords' – a restricted group of merchants – operated an exclusive trading patch at Glasgow Cross (*see page 49*). They must have been a colourful sight, dressed in traditional scarlet cloaks and black suits, and they were undoubtedly a powerful force both in Glasgow's economic and social life.

GLASGOW GREEN

Much-loved and much-used, Glasgow Green on the north bank of the River Clyde (*see page 125*) is one of the city's most historic sites. Over the years this huge village green in the centre of Glasgow has been used for an amazing mixture of purposes including common grazing, washing and bleaching linen and drying salmon nets! It has also been the scene of public hangings, military parades, public meetings, and a place where the wealthy would promenade with their families at weekends. Traditionally the property of all the people, it has long been the centre of merrymaking. The annual Glasgow Carnival (*see page 22*) still continues and while there are no longer swimming boxes or boxing booths, it is home for events such as the Glasgow Marathon (*see page 24*), Bonfire Night Spectacular (*see page 19*) the International Folk Festival (*see page 26*) and the Glasgow Cycling Grand Prix (*see page 23*).

The Green was described nearly 200 years ago as 'extremely valuable, considered as a place of exercise and where free air may at all time be enjoyed' and the same holds true today. It is a lovely place to wander through, a real joy so near the hustle and bustle of the city centre. The main feature is the People's Palace Museum (*see page 84*) but there are many other points of interest including: *Nelson Monument*, erected in 1806 by public subscription. Standing 144 feet (43m) high, it was the first monument to be built to the famous admiral in Great Britain; *Doulton's Fountain* with Queen Victoria at the summit, a strange earthenware statue built for the 1888 International Exhibition and moved to the Green in 1890; *James Watt Monument*, a plaque which marks the spot where Watt conceived the idea of the separate condenser for the steam engine; and to the east of the Green a large area known as *Fleshers' Haugh* used for playing football and boasting a pavilion which accommodates 460 players! (*See also walk 2*)

Open: all the time

EXTRA . . . EXTRA . . . James Watt was taking a stroll through the Green on a Sunday afternoon when he hit on the idea for a separate condenser in the steam engine, an invention which changed the course of history. He wrote to a friend, describing the events of the day: 'I had gone to take a walk on a fine Sabbath afternoon, early in 1765. I had entered the Green by the gate at the foot of Charlotte Street, and had passed the old washing house. I was thinking upon the engine at the time, and had gone as far as the herd's house, when the idea came into my mind that, as steam was an elastic body, it would rush into a vacuum, and if a communication were made between the cylinder and exhausted vessel, it would rush into it and might be condensed without cooling the cylinder . . . I had not walked further than the golf-house when the whole thing was arranged in my mind.'

HOGGANFIELD LOCH, Cumbernauld Road, Millerston (M8, Exit 12)

Don't be surprised if you spot a foolhardy swimmer braving the cold waters of this picturesque loch – it is a haven for watersports with boating and fishing becoming more and more popular. However, you don't have to be quite so active! The tree-lined path alongside the loch and open space all around makes a beautifully scenic place just to walk, picnic or sunbathe. The island in the centre is a bird sanctuary, so you should be able to see heron, wild duck and other species. There's also an aquarium where you can watch coarse fish – pike, perch, roach, bream, tench and so on – swimming at very close range, a treat for city children. It is a well-used place for a 'day out in the country' but don't be put off by the number of cars; you'll soon find your own spot away from the crowds. (*See also Triathlons at Hogganfield Loch, page 34).*

Open: all the time

EXTRA . . . EXTRA . . . To keep you up to date with the events taking place throughout the year in Glasgow's many parks and recreation facilities, the Department of Parks and Recreation produces a free *What's On* newsletter every month. For your copy contact them at 20 Trongate, Glasgow G1 5ES. Tel: 041-227 5116.

KELVIN WALKWAY – Dawsholm Road to Kelvingrove Park

Through woods and pretty parkland, up small hills, beside weirs and across bridges, the Kelvin Walkway which follows the gushing River Kelvin between Dawsholm Park (*see page 106*) and Kelvingrove Park (*see page 115*) runs for around 3 miles (4.8km) and makes a pleasant afternoon's stroll. The walk is particularly rich in wildlife – and look out for the willows growing by the waterside which provide cover for wildflowers such as the lesser Celandine with its beautiful yellow blossom. There's plenty of birdsong too, with the promise of an occasional appearance by a glorious kingfisher. You'll find lots of spots to enjoy a picnic, but a recommended resting point is beside the old North Woodside Flint Mill at Garrioch Mill Road. This partially restored mill, built in 1765, is a reminder of past industrial development along the banks of the Kelvin. Although today there's little evidence of this industrial heritage (with the notable exception of the unmistakable V-shaped weir that used to serve the Kelvinside paper mills) the walkway would once have been dotted with mills of all descriptions – mills for grinding flour and flint, paper mills, cotton mills and snuff mills. It is worth taking your time to enjoy the scenery along the way but remember, it is easy to get lost so keep the river clearly in view, and do wear stout shoes as it can be muddy at times.

Open: all the time

EXTRA ... EXTRA ... You can't miss the Great Aquaduct Bridge which carries the Forth and Clyde Canal (*see page 110*) across the Kelvin. When this four-arched bridge was built at the end of the 18th century, it was the largest of its kind in the world.

KELVINGROVE PARK, Kelvin Way

Kelvingrove Park is well worth a visit in its own right, but it is a particularly good place to know about if you are visiting some of Glasgow's major collections – the Hunterian Art Gallery (*see page 77*), Kelvingrove Art Gallery and Museum (*see page 79*), the Hunterian Museum (*see page 78*) or the Transport Museum (*see page 94*). Here you can have a picnic lunch beside an ornamental lake or amongst the park's abundant rhododendron blooms (best seen during May). Kelvingrove's 85 acres, laid out by Sir Joseph Paxton, are dotted with numerous statues, fountains and war memorials making it a fascinating place to walk on a sunny day. (*See also walk 3*)

Open: daily, dawn to dusk

EXTRA ... EXTRA ... The park is overlooked by Gilmorehill on which stands the distinctive tower of the University of Glasgow. The university was founded in 1451 and is the fourth oldest university in Britain.

KING'S PARK, Carmunnock Road

On a fine summer's day when the stocks, asters and sweet peas are in full bloom and the Highland cattle graze in the fields there can be few more pleasant spots than King's Park. Dotted with floral displays and some fine specimens of chestnut, lime, oak and yew trees, it is a lovely place for a leisurely walk or picnic. One of the main features is the walled garden which has recently been restored and replanted. This was once the kitchen garden for the mansion house and used to grow vegetables and fruit with greenhouses full of figs, grapes and indoor fruits. Today it is a colourful show of heathers and herbaceous plants. The mansion house, called Aikenhead House, is now private housing. Built in the mid-17th century it was rebuilt in 1806 and the wings added in 1823. It is floodlit at night and the rose-coloured sandstone makes an attractive picture night and day. Look out for the unusual-shaped sundial in the middle of the flower lawn. Classed as a listed structure, it originally stood in the formal garden of Douglas Castle, Lanarkshire. For a free nature-trail leaflet around King's Park contact The Countryside Ranger Service, Mansion House, Linn Park, Glasgow G44 5TA. Tel: 041-637 1147.

Open: all the time

EXTRA . . . EXTRA . . . Don't leave without saying hello to two of the park's most popular residents – Angus, the rare Eriskey stallion and Darky, the Highland Pony. You'll see them grazing in the fields with the Highland cattle.

LINN PARK, Clarkston Road

One of the most attractive features of this 220-acre country park is, without doubt, the fast-flowing White Cart River with its dramatic change of pace and beautiful waterfall. To enjoy it to the full, follow the riverside walkway, a circular walk between the White Cart Bridge and the old snuff mill which, if you take it at a leisurely pace enjoying the countryside, takes around an hour and a half. This park, the end of a finger of green which runs from the Fenwick Moors, is so peaceful and well clothed by trees it is almost impossible to believe you're only a few miles from the centre of Glasgow. Indeed, as you stand on the old 17th-century bridge, once part of the main stage-coach route from Glasgow to Kilmarnock, you can almost hear the clatter of the horses' hooves as they speed along. Natural and unspoilt, it is just the place to come for that 'away from it all' feeling. However, if you're looking for something a little more sociable, you can wander around the children's zoo, modest admittedly, but all the animals are very friendly and used to being stroked. There's also a visitor centre in the mansion house with a nature and information room where you can find out all about the wildlife in the park. And if you fancy some refreshment, everyone is welcome in the tea room where you can enjoy the sweeping view of the golf course. For a free nature trail leaflet and details of free guided walks around the park for individuals and groups contact: Countryside Ranger Service, Mansion House, Linn Park, Glasgow G44 5TA. Tel: 041-637 1147.

Open: all the time

EXTRA . . . EXTRA . . . At the southern end of the park are the ruins of Cathcart Castle which dates back to the times of William Wallace and Robert the Bruce. Nearby on the small hill known as 'Court Knowe' is a plaque which marks the spot where, on 13 May 1568, Mary Queen of Scots is said to have watched her army's defeat at the Battle of Langside (*see also Queen's Park, page 124*). Many people say they've seen the ghost of Mary haunting the site, so tread with care!

MUGDOCK COUNTRY PARK, Milngavie (off A81)

A brisk walk from the railway station at Milngavie (pronounced Milguy) takes you up a steep hill to this huge 500-acre country park which stretches nearly all the way to Strathblane – indeed, the two are separated only by a ¾-

acre stretch of open moorland. It is tempting to take the bus to the top of the hill but the beautiful views over lochs and woodland make the effort of walking well worthwhile, especially as there are stopping points to rest and take photographs. The road, the starting point of the arduous West Highland Way (*see page 133*), leads upwards past the beginning of Drumclog Moor on the left and then Mugdock Reservoir on the right (another favourite place for a country walk) until you come to the South Lodge access to the park on your left. It's a real mixture of parkland, woods, marshes, moors, lochs and pastures, all bustling with wildlife, with plenty of places to explore – look out for the remains of two castles, Mugdock Castle and Craigend Castle. There's a ranger service based at the park which organizes activities, talks and walks for children and adults, highlighting the natural history such as the fungus harvest on Drumclog Moor or the butterflies and dragonflies that live around Mugdock Loch. To find out more call in at the visitor centre at Craigend Stables, near Craigend Castle, or contact the rangers at: Craigend Stables Visitor Centre, Mugdock Country Park, Craigallion Road, Milngavie. Tel: 041-956 6100.

Open: daily, dawn to dusk

EXTRA . . . EXTRA . . . The Mugdock Conservation Volunteers are always looking for new recruits to help with jobs such as felling and planting trees and building bridges. They get together on a number of Saturday mornings throughout the year to work in the park. No skills or tools are needed, just enthusiasm. The ranger service (*see above*) will tell you more.

MUIRSHIEL COUNTRY PARK (off A760).
Tel: Lochwinnoch 842 803

If you don't have a car it will take some effort to reach
Muirshiel Country Park, but do try – you'll be well
rewarded! Park seems something of a misnomer for this
far from domestic landscape. There are the usual country
park facilities – car park, toilets, ranger centre – but as
soon as you begin to walk you'll find youself in a wild and
spectacular environment. If you are coming by public
transport, the bus or train will drop you at the village of
Lochwinnoch then it's a four-mile hike following the
single track road up the Calder Glen. It is a beautiful
walk as the valley is an impressive groove cut into the
moorland plateau. Muirshiel Country Park once belonged
to Muirshiel estate whose grounds were taken from the
wild moor some 200 years ago. There's so much to see
and do that you definitely should allow a whole day (with
a packed lunch) for a visit. If you're keen on fishing,
obtain a free day permit from the ranger; if you're
interested in fauna and flora, try following one of the two
main trails, 'Country Trail' or 'Habitat Trail'. There's
plenty to spot: stoat, weasel, field vole, pigmy shrew, roe
deer, buzzard, kestrel, sparrow hawk; St John's wort,
monkey flower and musk. (*See also Renfrew page 157*)

Open: park: all the time; information centre: daily, mid-
October–start of British summer time, 0900–1630;
summer, 0830–dusk

EXTRA . . . EXTRA . . . Some people visit the park
for a rather macabre reason – to seek out crashed aircraft.
Muirshiel used to be the first high land reached by aircraft
approaching from the west (flight paths have since
changed) and there were numerous crashes in poor visi-

bility. The wrecked remains of aircraft dating back to 1930 can still be seen.

OVERTOUN PARK, Mill Street, Rutherglen

There's always something going on in this busy 12-acre park at the centre of Rutherglen, whether it is people taking a gentle stroll with their dogs, or the sporty enjoying more active pursuits: there are tennis courts, a putting green, bowling greens and table-tennis units. The floral displays are quite spectacular too – indeed, they have become quite famous for their colourful and imaginative use of plants. But as well as providing you with lots of things to see and do, the park is also beautifully situated and a lovely, relaxing place to wander around. Adjoining is the rather more secluded Woodburn Park; peaceful and wooded, it's a perfect place for a country walk. (*See also Rutherglen Museum, page 89*)

Open: all the time

EXTRA . . . EXTRA . . . The wide, tree-lined Main Street of Rutherglen is now a busy shopping area but until 1900 it was an important centre for horse and cattle fairs.

POLLOK COUNTRY PARK, Main entrance, 2060 Pollokshaws Road. Tel: 041-227 5065

Pollok Country Park is really huge, some 361 acres. It contains extensive natural woodland, a unique collection of trees and shrubs, beautiful Pollok House (*see page 85*) and the stunning, world famous Burrell Collection (*see page 71*). And all this is to be enjoyed just three miles south of Glasgow city centre. You can't fail to find plenty to do and see in the park, but it may help to know about some of its attractions.

Countryside Ranger Centre (*see page 74*).

Earthwork – an ancient earth bank and ditch can be seen near the Demonstration Garden (*see below*).

Mediaeval Ringwork – you'll have to be very observant to spot this indistinct site near North Wood.

Suspension Bridge – where the river bends near Pollok Cricket Club you can see the metal straining posts for the bridge which was demolished in the 1960s.

North Lodge – built in 1892, the cottage wall bears the Maxwell family motto, 'I am ready gang forward'.

Icehouse – a shallow circular shaft remains. From around 1650 the practice of storing ice for use in spring and summer began to spread to the wealthier estates of Britain. The ice was stored in a pit lined with blocks of stone, its roof, which was at ground level, was covered with turf.

Curling Pond – this was constructed in the late 19th century.

Dovecote – dates from the 17th century when pigeons provided a valuable source of fresh meat during the winter months. (*See also walk 4*)

Open: Daily, 0800–dusk

EXTRA . . . EXTRA . . . Pollok's history is that of a 700-year occupation by one family – the Maxwells. The earliest castle was built here by Sir John Maxwell when he became owner of Pollok in the 13th century.

POLLOK DEMONSTRATION GARDEN,
Pollok Country Park, Pollokshaws Road.
Tel: 041-632 9299

Part of Pollok Country Park (*see page 121*), the Demonstration Garden is nevertheless well worth visiting in its own right. Situated within the walled garden of Pollok House (*see page 85*) the Demonstration Garden covers two acres and you don't have to be a professional to enjoy what it has to offer. At the garden you might pick up ideas on landscaping, discover how to use arches, gates and paths, learn about varying kinds of hedge and ground-cover plants. There's a pretty herb garden, colourful herbaceous borders and, to help bring the past to life, a restored 'Gardeners' Bothy'. This small house, now a museum displaying early gardening tools and implements, was in 1900, home for the estate gardener. (*See also walk 4 and Lectures (gardening talks) page 29*)

Open: Monday–Thursday, 0800–1600; Friday, 0800–1500; weekends–summer, 0800–1830; winter, 0800–1600

EXTRA . . . EXTRA . . . If you're green-fingered but have gardening problems you might like to make use of the Gardening Advice Phone-In Service. Whatever your gardening question the experts will try and help: Tel: 041-632 9299, Thursday, 1400–1600.

QUEEN'S PARK, Langside Road

A strange collection of stones near the flagpole at the highest point of the park is a reminder of the history of what is now Queen's Park, named after Mary Queen of Scots. It is thought that the Battle of Langside, where Mary's army was defeated in 1568, was fought on these slopes and the stones may well be remains of a military encampment made during the battle. Whether the story is true or not, the circle of stones is certainly always popular with children playing at soldiers! The park itself is well defined into the natural south side and the more formal north side. The latter, designed by Sir Joseph Paxton and laid out in grand Victorian style, is famed for its fine floral displays throughout the year. Whether you prefer the grassy slopes and woodland of the south or the formal gardens of the north, you can always be sure of lovely views of the surrounding countryside.

Open: daily, dawn to dusk

EXTRA . . . EXTRA . . . Outside the Battle Place entrance to the park there's a 58-foot-high (18.5m) column which commemorates the Battle of Langside, 13 May 1568. The battle, fought here just 11 days after Mary's escape from Loch Leven, saw her defeat by Moray. She is believed to have watched the battle from 'Court Knowe' in Linn Park (*see page 117*).

RICHMOND PARK, Shawfield Drive

A pleasant way to approach Richmond Park is from Glasgow Green (*see page 112*). Just cross over Polmadie Bridge and you're there! The 44-acre park is bordered on one side by Rutherglen Road and on the other by the winding River Clyde (*see below*), setting for many a summer rowing event. Although the main flower gardens run parallel to Rutherglen Road and are usually a feast of colour, the most interesting part of the park is beside the river. Here, little pathways and hidden features make it a great place to explore. A favourite for children is the pond at the centre where swans and waterfowl are always on the lookout for a tasty morsel. There's also a putting green, bowling green and cricket pitch.

Open: all the time

EXTRA . . . EXTRA . . . You'll find a fine example of a typical Glaswegian Victorian red-sandstone tenement block in Rutherglen Road, now cleaned and restored.

RIVER CLYDE

They say that Glasgow made the Clyde and the Clyde made Glasgow and, indeed, it was this winding river which flows through the city and opens into the Firth of Clyde, one of the greatest harbours in the world, that helped establish Glasgow's great trading tradition and later launched many of the greatest ever liners. You can walk along the north side of the river between Victoria Bridge and the Scottish Exhibition and Conference Centre, host to the 1988 Glasgow Garden Festival. The walkway takes you along Custom House Quay (*see page 105*), under Kingston Bridge, along Anderston Quay and Lancefield Quay to Finnieston Quay (look out for the massive Finnieston crane) and Stobcross Quay and finally to the exhibition centre. If you're in Glasgow in July or August, you might catch sight of the restored *Waverley*, the last sea-going paddle steamer in the world taking visitors along the river. (*See also Regattas, page 33 and walk 2*)

Open: all the time

EXTRA . . . EXTRA . . . The Festival Bridge, a 360-foot (120m) swing-bridge which pivots on a central tower to allow ships to pass through, is the first footbridge to be built over the River Clyde in nearly 100 years.

ROSSHALL PARK, Crookston Road

No expense spared. . . that was the brief given to landscape gardeners back in the early 1900s when the Cowan family decided to turn their estate at Rosshall Park into a garden of exceptional beauty with lakes, waterfalls and grottoes. The garden has been extended and changed over the years but it is still a beautiful place to visit. Completely free of any recreational facilities, it is a real haven for nature lovers – a combination of a garden where many rare and unusual plants and flowers grow and an area of natural scenery with wooded paths leading down to the fast-flowing River Cart (*see also Linn Park, page 117*). So forget the football and bring the binoculars instead!

Open: daily, dawn to dusk

EXTRA . . . EXTRA . . . You can follow the River Cart from Crookston Road to Corkerhill Road along the White Cart Walkway. The walk takes you through Lochar Park, an attractive 15-acre park set within a winding loop of the river.

ROUKEN GLEN PARK, Rouken Glen Road

Ask any Glaswegian about Rouken Glen Park and they'll delight in describing the beauty of the waterfall. Indeed, it is a truly spectacular sight as the shimmering water of Auldhouse Burn tumbles over a precipice at the head of the glen. You can spend hours admiring the changing shades of colour as light catches the cascading water. The park, just five miles from the city centre, covers 228 acres and as much is left in its natural state there are lovely walks through woodland. However, there are also more formal areas: a boating pond, an alpine house with a fine collection of rare plants, and a much-acclaimed walled garden with well over 100,000 plants. And if you're lucky you might well spot some St Mungo Highland cattle grazing by the side of the golf course. But it is the waterfall you'll remember and talk about for days after!

Open: daily, dawn to dusk

EXTRA . . . EXTRA . . . Near the entrance on Thornliebank Road at the Thornliebank Gate is an ivy-grown façade. This is the remains of the mansion of Birkenshaw where Lord Kelvin, pioneer in electrical engineering, once lived.

RUCHILL PARK, Firhill Road

The highlight of a trip to this 52-acre park is the view from the artificial mound known as 'Ben Whitton' after the man in charge of the Parks Department when it was constructed. Climb the mound to the flagpole on the summit and you'll be rewarded with some quite beautiful scenery; in the foreground there's a good all-round view of the city with its church spires, trees and cemeteries and far in the distance the Campsie Fells (*see page 102*) and Ben Lomond. It is a rather steep walk but don't worry – there's a seat at the top! The park is also noted for its summer bedding displays – the dahlias and begonias are much admired.

Open: all the time

EXTRA . . . EXTRA . . . It took 24,000 cartloads of material to make the mound!

SIGHTHILL PARK, Pinkston Road (off Baird Street)

Don't be surprised if you can't find this park on your map – it was only opened in 1982 as a result of land reclamation and is still little known. A fascinating feature is the reconstructed megalith site with 'time capsule' – a sort of mini-Stonehenge that makes a great play area for children and a perfect picnic spot. The site also offers views over the city – look especially for Sighthill Cemetery, just half a mile to the north. It's a wonderful hotch-potch of wind- and weather-battered gravestones. Among them is the 'Martyrs' Memorial' which marks the graves of Andrew

Hardie and John Baird, who were hanged and beheaded at Stirling for their part in the attempted workers' revolt of 1820. To bring you back to the present, the park is a favourite spot for joggers so you'll probably see a few enthusiastic keep-fitters on their way to the trim track!

Open: all the time

EXTRA . . . EXTRA . . . The southern boundary of the park marks the line of the old Monklands Canal and the route of Scotland's first passenger railway line, the Glasgow to Garnkirk, which had its terminus just west of Pinkston Road.

SPRINGBURN PARK, Broomfield Road

Set in one of the highest areas of north Glasgow, the park rises to 351 feet (107m) at its highest point (by the water tower near the Winter Gardens) and, as you'd imagine, the views are superb. The park covers 78 acres and, having an impressive number of facilities, it is always busy. There are three bowling greens, tennis courts, a putting green and pitches for football, hockey and cricket so you can be sure to get an afternoon's entertainment watching sport! For children there's a paddle-boat pond. You'll also find displays of flowers throughout the seasons and two ponds where waterfowl live and breed. While you're in the area, it is worth visiting the Springburn Museum (*see page 91*) which has displays on the history of Springburn.

Open: daily, dawn to dusk

EXTRA . . . EXTRA . . . Weather recordings have been taken at Springburn Park since 1896. The staff operate a small weather station gathering in weather data 365 days a year to be sent to the Meteorological Office in Edinburgh.

TOLLCROSS PARK, Wellshot Road

A green haven in the midst of Glasgow's industrial east end, Tollcross Park is always a favourite with children who love the Children's Zoo here. The goats, rabbits, sheep, ponies and other inhabitants are all friendly and positively adore being stroked, so don't be shy! The park, originally the grounds of Tollcross House, a fine Victorian mansion designed in 1848 by David Bryce, the great master of Victorian country house design, is well laid out with lawns, trees and lively displays of flowers – there's even a bubbling stream running through.

Open: daily, dawn to dusk

EXTRA . . . EXTRA . . . Within the park there are trial beds for new varieties of roses. This is where new strains are grown and tested so you can not only get a sneak preview of what's going to be in your garden in a few seasons' time but also the chance to see a beautiful mass of different roses from past years of all colours and shapes.

TORRANCE DEMONSTRATION AND ORNAMENTAL GARDENS, Campsie Road, Torrance

Growing herbs, gardening to encourage wildlife, starting summer flowers from seed, choosing outdoor flowers for floral arrangements – these are just a few of the many and varied horticultural demonstrations organized for green-fingered enthusiasts at these beautifully presented gardens every year. The demonstrations, which are held on certain Saturday mornings from March to November, last around an hour and a half and everyone is welcome to come along, there is no need to book in advance. Whether you're a complete amateur or a keen expert you'll find it an educative and entertaining way of spending a Saturday morning. But you don't have to go to a demonstration; the gardens are open all year round and there's always something of interest to see. (*See also Strathkelvin, page 158*)

Open: gardens: Monday–Thursday, 0800–1630; Friday 0800–1530. Demonstrations held on Saturdays from 1030 to 1200 (Demonstration Garden open at 1000 for viewing and questions). For dates and topics contact: Parks and Cemeteries Department, 14 Springfield Road, Bishopbriggs. Tel: 041-772 3210

EXTRA . . . EXTRA . . . Gadloch, a real haven for wildlife is just two miles away. Although it is particularly popular with bird spotters (you can often see Hooper swans here in the autumn), the shores of the loch also abound with wildflowers.

VICTORIA PARK, Victoria Park Drive North, Whiteinch

The most popular feature of Victoria Park is undoubtedly the Fossil Grove with perfect fossils of tree stumps dating back an incredible 330 million years. But the park itself, despite its closeness to the busy Clyde Expressway and Clyde Tunnel, is one of the most beautiful in Glasgow. Covering some 58 acres, with tall trees giving an air of seclusion and tranquillity, there's a flower garden with holly-lined bays, a model boating pond, an arboretum, and a colourful rock garden which seems to have a cheerful display of flowers whatever the season. The Fossil Grove, now housed in a glass-roofed building, was discovered by workmen in 1887 when they were digging a pathway across a disused whinstone quarry. They weren't quite sure what they'd found, but they realized the strange-looking objects were of importance and called in the experts. What they had uncovered were the fossilized remains of an ancient Carboniferous forest – the tree stumps and roots had been preserved by mud and shale beds and gradually turned to stone. There's a viewing gallery in the Fossil Grove building so you can look down on the fossilized stumps and roots of these primitive trees. It's an incredible and unique sight – don't miss it!

Open: variable, but usually daily, 0900–1600

EXTRA ... EXTRA ... The trees which grew in Carboniferous forests millions of years ago became the source of the Clydeside coal which was so important for industrial development along the River Clyde.

THE WEST HIGHLAND WAY, Milngavie to Fort William

Tough, rough and strenuous, the West Highland Way is a challenge few dedicated hill walkers can resist. It runs for 95 miles (152 km) northwards from Milngavie to Fort William and usually takes about a week to complete, depending, of course, on the highly unpredictable Scottish weather conditions! For the less hardy, there are several short stretches within the route which are easy going but to get the full variety of scenery and wildlife along the way you need to tackle every step. You'll walk along historic paths, using drove roads by which the Highlanders herded their cattle to the Lowlands; 18th-century military roads; old coaching roads, farm tracks and disused railway lines. You'll follow the shores of Loch Lomond, Britain's largest and arguably most beautiful loch and eventually arrive at the foot of Ben Nevis, Britain's highest mountain, which stands some 4406 feet (1344m) high. Inexperienced walkers are warned not even to try and attempt it, but if you're used to trekking up and down rugged mountainland and across desolate moors, then you'll enjoy the West Highland Way. For a free leaflet with general information and a list of places to stay en route contact: Countryside Commission for Scotland, Battleby, Redgorton, Perth PH1 3EW.

Open: all the time

EXTRA ... EXTRA ... While in Milngavie, don't miss the Lillie Art Gallery (Tel: 041-956 2351), a modern gallery with a permanent collection of 20th-century Scottish paintings, sculpture and ceramics, and temporary exhibitions throughout the year.

CHAPTER FIVE
Places of Work

AUCTIONS

The variety of things that come under the hammer at auction houses in Glasgow is quite amazing – everything from cigarette cards and teddy bears to antique silver and jewellery, and when they can be found, the work of Scottish designers such as Charles Rennie Mackintosh (*see page 52*), Christopher Dresser and Jessie King. Sales are held regularly during the week and everyone is welcome – dealers, enthusiasts and just curious onlookers. It is fascinating to watch, but don't wave your arms around too much or you may find yourself going home with more than you'd bargained for! Telephone first to find out the dates and times of the sales, or look in the *Glasgow Herald (see page 146)* on Monday for the weekly listing.

Here are three of the leading auction houses:

Ashby's, 8 Cresswell Lane. Tel: 041-339 8240

Christie's & Edmiston's Ltd. 164–166 Bath Street. Tel: 041-332 8134/7

Phillips, 207 Bath Street. Tel: 041-221 8377

EXTRA ... EXTRA ... If you're interested in antiques and fine arts, you'll have hours of pleasure browsing around the many shops and galleries in Glasgow. For a full list pick up the free information sheet, Antiques and Fine Art Dealers, from the Greater Glasgow Tourist Board, 39 St Vincent Place. Tel: 041-227 4885

CONSERVATION: CLYDE REGION ENVIRONMENTAL WORKERS (CREW)

Treeplanting, restoring drystone dykes, building mountain paths and managing woodlands – these are just a few of the many practical conservation projects in and around Glasgow carried out by CREW, a group of volunteers aged between 16 and 70. They're a friendly and committed team working all year round to protect the environment for the future and they're always on the lookout for helping hands. If you'd like to find out a little more about their activities, why not join one of their working days? To become a member of CREW there's a nominal charge but you're welcome to support and encourage for free – just bring along your own sandwiches for lunch.

Further information from: Chris Melling, CREW, 99 Bowman Street, Glasgow G42 8LE. Tel: 041-423 7204 (evening)

EXTRA . . . EXTRA . . . One of CREW's projects is a tree nursery. Seeds from trees or shrubs growing wild in Scotland can be collected – for free – and grown in the nursery. They'll offer advice on the best ways of collecting and keeping seeds.

COUNCIL MEETINGS, City Chambers.
Tel: 041-227 4017

The public can attend meetings of Glasgow District Council held in the Council Hall in City Chambers (*see page 42*) where a special gallery gives a good view of the proceedings. The meetings are held every four weeks to make plans and discuss the affairs of the council over the previous four weeks. The debates, which vary in length from half an hour to a full afternoon, can sometimes be a trifle tedious, especially for a visitor to Glasgow, but it is a marvellous opportunity to get a really good look at the magnificent mahogany-panelled hall. Don't forget to look up to enjoy the central dome decorated with delicate stained glass.

Open: meetings are held at 1330 on every fourth Thursday. Admission is by ticket only, obtainable from the City Chambers. Telephone or write in advance

---

EXTRA . . . EXTRA . . . The Lord Provost's chair was a present from Queen Victoria at the formal opening of the building in 1888.

CRAFT WORKSHOPS, Quarrier's Village, Bridge of Weir (off A761)

Quarrier's Village – a picturesque group of some 50 cottages in Bridge of Weir – was founded in 1871 by William Quarrier. Then it was a haven for some 500 orphaned or destitute children; today it's being developed for private housing and craft workshops. Some of the craft workers are happy to show visitors their crafts and techniques.

Dormouse Designs The Old Drapery, Faith Avenue
Sue Quin designs and manufactures award-winning soft toys. Here, in her workshop, you can make the acquaintance of characters such as Bramble Bear, a very special bear who has his own wardrobe of clothes. Then there's School Hare, a delightful individual dressed in a hand-

knitted sweater, cotton poplin shirt, grey school trousers and a pure-wool, felt blazer. He carries a real leather school bag and even has a carrot for playtime! These toys are really collectors' items and they come with a certificate of authenticity. You can see the effort which goes into creating each one – the fabrics are marked out and cut by hand, then sewn, stuffed and assembled. There's certainly plenty for a visitor to learn including what it means when a piece of material 'shows its teeth'!

Open: Monday–Friday, 1000–1600

Lorend Knitwear In this small workshop you can see wool transformed from strands wrapped on a cone into a brightly coloured sweater. The place is alive with activity as hand-framed knitting machines, linking machines and even washing machines seem in continuous use. Then there's the labelling and packing; you can see it all. But remember, it is a working environment and people may be just too busy to stop and explain what they're doing.

Open: by prior appointment only. Tel: Bridge of Weir 613322

Village Pottery A real cottage industry; the husband-and-wife team who run Village Pottery produce ceramic mirror and picture frames, terracotta figures, fantasy castles and a range of crofters' cottages. If you want to know how the objects are made, all you have to do is ask!

Open: Monday–Friday (except Tuesday and Friday afternoons), 0930–1600

EXTRA . . . EXTRA . . . The hand of Charles Rennie Mackintosh (*see page 52*) can be seen in Bridge of Weir; take a look at the façade of 'Easterhill' in Bankend Road.

GLASGOW AIRPORT, Abbotsinch, Nr. Paisley. Tel: 041-887 1111

Opened by the Queen in 1966, Glasgow airport has since become quite an attraction for local people. Enthusiasts, armed with binoculars, spend whole afternoons plane-spotting. Bins or not, you can enjoy the excellent view of planes landing, taxiing and taking off. It is perhaps a good time to remember the saying that Glasgow is 'the little country' where 'every visit is like coming home'.

Open: all the time

EXTRA . . . EXTRA . . . The airport, now Britain's third busiest, was developed from the former Royal National Air Station at Abbotsinch.

GLASGOW PRINT STUDIO – WORKSHOP, 22 King Street. Tel: 041-552 0704

When you've seen an exhibition in the Glasgow Print Studio's gallery, it is interesting to visit its workshop and see the techniques behind the art. The workshop may be a bit tatty round the edges, but it is full of atmosphere and anyone making a print – relief, silk screen, etching or lithograph – will enthusiastically show you what they're doing.

Open: Monday–Saturday, 1000–1730 (ask in the gallery first)

EXTRA . . . EXTRA . . . The workshop provides facilities which are used by some 200 people. The printmakers are mainly from the west of Scotland, but Glasgow Print Studio is increasingly gaining international recognition with artists from as far away as Australia travelling to Glasgow to share the creative environment it provides.

GLASGOW ROYAL MAIL, 400 Paisley Road. Tel: 041-242 4100

As late as 1715 the Glasgow-to-Edinburgh postal service was still carried out on foot. What's more, mail from London was routed, much to the annoyance of Glaswegians, via the Scottish capital, Edinburgh. All very different from today's organization; in Glasgow's present bang-up-to-date mechanized letter office (MLO) some 5½ million items of post make their way through the system each week. Much of it is sorted automatically with each operator being expected to process at least 1600 letters an hour. It is best to visit the MLO during the evening when you can get a really good idea of the enormous scale of the operation. But whenever you take a tour you'll get to see a short film and be treated to coffee and biscuits as well as being offered the chance to air your views on the efficiency of the postal service.

Open: by arrangement only, daily from 1400 (best 1730)

EXTRA . . . EXTRA . . . 'Not proven' is a verdict only to be heard in a Scottish court. It means that a jury believes that a defendant is probably guilty but feels that there is insufficient evidence to prove the case. This was the verdict given at the famous trial of Madeleine Smith who was thought to have poisoned her lover, Pierre

Emile. The date on a crucial letter which would have proved her guilt was indecipherable – the controller of the sorting office was called in, but the postmark had been carelessly struck. Madeleine lived on to the ripe old age of 93 and the Glasgow post office was subjected to a total reorganization by one Anthony Trollope.

GREATER POSSIL CITY FARM, Ellesmere Street, Hamiltonhill. Tel: 041-336 8754

Geese, ducks, ponies, rabbits, pet lambs and bantams . . . you'll find them all down on the farm. This six-acre plot of land near Possil Cross is Glasgow's first inner-city farm designed to give urban dwellers, both children and adults, a taste of country life. There's a wonderfully informal atmosphere with visitors welcome just to wander around, meet the animals and admire the flowers in the wildlife garden, or, if you're feeling energetic, all help is gratefully received. Perhaps you could muck out the goats (but be warned – they always seem to be up to some sort of mischief), dig up a few weeds in the allotments or collect some freshly laid eggs. Special events are held throughout the year.

Open: daily, 0900–dusk

EXTRA . . . EXTRA . . . For more farmyard animals in the city, head for Glasgow Green (*see page 112*). Although no longer used for grazing, the green is a favourite exercise ground for the award-winning Clydesdale horses owned by the Glasgow Parks Department and used for publicity purposes. You'll see them out most afternoons, and if you ask, you might be given a sneak look at their stables too.

THE HIGH COURT, Jocelyn Square.
Tel: 041-552 0317

It is here in this Grecian Justiciary Building that criminal cases are brought to trial. There are two courts – the South Court and North Court and both have public galleries where you can just sit and look down on the proceedings below. And even if the actual case isn't particularly exciting, it is always interesting to see justice in action. The attendants on duty outside are well clued up on what is on where and when so it is worth talking to them first. The building itself was designed by William Stark in 1814 and served as the City Chambers until 1844. (*See also walk 2*)

Open: Monday–Friday, 1000–1300, 1400–1600

EXTRA . . . EXTRA . . . Jocelyn Square, once known as Jail Square, was the site of public hangings until 1865.

IBROX STADIUM Edmiston Drive.
Tel: 041-427 5232

If you've ever cheered Rangers on, either from the stands or from the comfort of your armchair, why not pay their home – Ibrox Stadium – a visit? You can see the pitch (without the players!), the dressing room and maybe even see the 'lads' training. But most impressive of all is the

Trophy Room. Here, six glass cases are packed with trophies awarded over the years to Rangers, while the walls and beams of the room are festooned with pennants from football teams across the world. A whole wall is devoted to framed presentation cloths won by Rangers in League Championships. All the exhibits are very well kept, but they're presented without much labelling – so you need to know your stuff!

Open: you may be allowed to see the Trophy Room without booking, but it is best to make sure and join a guided tour. To arrange a tour write to the Secretary (address above)

EXTRA . . . EXTRA . . . Glasgow's two rival football teams were founded on Fleshers' Haugh, Glasgow Green (*see page 112*): Rangers (1873) and Celtic (1888).

MORRISON'S AUCHENTOSHAN DISTILLERY, Dalmuir. Tel: Duntocher 78561

Auchentoshan is one of the oldest licensed distilleries in Scotland and has two main claims to fame – firstly it uses a triple distillation process (all other whiskies are distilled twice) using three separate stills. And secondly, it produces an award-winning Lowland malt whisky. Made from water drawn from Loch Cochno, which is lightly peated, and mashed in a special way, the whisky – as you may well taste for yourself – has a unique flavour. Unfortunately, the tour of this famous distillery is rather brief, lasting only 20–25 minutes, and the noise so overpowering you can hardly hear your guide. However, the introductory talk beforehand fills you in on all the background information and the free sampling afterwards leaves you with a warm and pleasant glow.

Open: to book, write or telephone well in advance

EXTRA . . . EXTRA . . . Auchentoshan means 'Corner of the Field' in Gaelic. Although now surrounded by an industrial estate, the distillery, when it was originally built in 1823, stood in the corner of a field where barley grew, the essence of malt whisky.

NEWSPAPER: GLASGOW HERALD AND EVENING TIMES, 195 Albion Street.
Tel: 041-552 6255

It is noisy, dirty and quite exhausting – but a guided tour of the *Glasgow Herald* and *Evening Times* is absolutely enthralling! You're taken through all the different processes and shown exactly how a newspaper is put together – through the editorial and advertising offices to the process department, composing room, platemaking department, press room and finally the circulation and despatch departments. Just don't expect anyone, except your guide, to stop and talk to you – there are deadlines to meet! Indeed, there's an almost frenetic atmosphere – people rushing here and there, instant decisions, telephones ringing and machines humming – until everyone breathes a sigh of relief at 2230 and a calm descends as you watch the first newspapers start rolling off the presses. You'll read your free copy with a new respect, and a lot more insight into the tricks of the trade! The tour can be rather technical at times and so it is not recommended for children under 12.

Open: by appointment only. Tours run from September to May on Tuesday evenings, 1930–2230. Interested groups (up to 20) are welcome; to arrange a tour telephone the Personnel Department, then confirm in writing. Individuals can usually join an organized party. But be warned, tours are very popular and are often booked up to a year in advance.

EXTRA . . . EXTRA . . . For printed matter of a different era make your way to Cooper Hay Rare Books, 203 Bath Street. Tel: 041-226 3074 (open: Monday–Friday, 1000–1700; Saturday, 1000–1300). The shelves are lined with leather-bound books and the atmosphere is wonderfully studious.

POTTERY: SALTOUN POTTERY, 24 Ruthven Street. Tel: 041-334 4240

Housed in a wooden garage down a narrow lane, this pottery is full of unexpected delights and has a very welcoming atmosphere. The extensive range of ceramic goods on sale is probably the first thing you notice and, as you'll soon discover, this is a result of moving from hand-throwing pots using age-old traditional craft skills to more modern methods. It is fascinating watching the potters at work producing porcelain and stoneware and they're happy to answer your questions, so do ask about the different techniques. (*See also walk 3*)

Open: all year, Tuesday–Sunday, 1000–1730

EXTRA . . . EXTRA . . . Nearby in Huntly Gardens is the impressive Kelvinside-Hillhead Parish Church, designed by James Sellars in 1875 with a Sainte-Chapelle theme.

SEWERAGE IN STRATHCLYDE

A visit to a sewage works and pumping station makes a very unusual tour. For safety reasons you're not allowed underground to see the sewers, but you can take a look at the circular sedimentation tanks. The Department of Sewerage also operates sludge-disposal vessels and one of them – MV *Garroch Head* – takes passengers.

Dates: tours of the works and pumping station are arranged for groups only and must be booked well in advance. Trips on the sludge boat take place twice weekly during the summer months – but they're very popular, so apply well in advance Write to: Department of Sewerage, Strathclyde House, 20 India Street, Glasgow G2 4PF

EXTRA . . . EXTRA . . . Some facts about Strathclyde's sewerage system: it has some 7,000 miles (11,270km) of sewers; 179 pumping stations; a massive 240 million gallons are pumped every day; it has 142 sewage treatment works.

STAINED GLASS: LEADLINE STUDIO, Unit N16, Clyde Workshops, Fullarton Road, Tollcross. Tel: 041-641 0610

It is a bit of a trek out to the Clyde Workshops, but you can be sure that Shona McInnes will give you a warm welcome to her small stained-glass studio. And once she starts explaining and demonstrating all the stages from the initial design through the various techniques – staining, painting, etching, cutting, firing, leading and soldering, you'll find the journey will have been well worth it. Shona receives all kinds of different commissions, and as well as designing and making new windows and panels for houses and churches she does a lot of restoration work. As you can imagine, she's very busy, but telephone in advance and she'll be more than happy to show you around (maximum number 6). Allow around half an hour for your visit, but don't leave without asking to see her portfolio – it is quite sparkling!

Open: by appointment only. Monday, Wednesday–Saturday, 1000–1800

EXTRA . . . EXTRA . . . Glasgow prides itself on its tradition in fine stained glass and there's a beautiful collection, from 1850 to 1940, in The People's Palace (*see page 84*).

THE STOCK EXCHANGE, Nelson Mandela Place (formerly St George's Place).
Tel: 041-221 7060

It is worth enjoying the Gothic beauty of the building from the outside before you go indoors. Although extensively rebuilt and refurbished in 1971, the external walls, designed by John Burnet, 1875–7, are still intact and are an outstanding example of Venetian Gothic architecture. Once inside, make your way up to the Visitors' Gallery where you'll get a bird's-eye view of the proceedings on the trading floor. Today, it is a very quiet affair with everyone seated at desks and a notable lack of all the shouting and calling once associated with the daily business of the stock exchange, but don't be deceived: the buying and selling is just as busy – and as confusing for newcomers – as ever! To give you some idea of what is going on, pick up the free leaflets in the Visitors' Gallery which explain the history, practice and some of the traditions. (*See also walk 1*)

Open: Monday–Friday, 1000–1245, 1400–1530

EXTRA . . . EXTRA . . . The South African Consulate has its offices in the Stock Exchange Chambers and in 1986 Glasgow District Council renamed the Place 'Nelson Mandela Place'.

STRATHCLYDE POLICE DOG TRAINING CENTRE, Pollok Country Park, Pollokshaws Road.

If you've ever admired the work police dogs do, take the opportunity to see them being put through their paces. At the dog-training centre in Pollok Country Park (*see page 121*) you can watch an impressive display. There's also the chance to tour the centre's buildings and kennels.

Open: usually Tuesday mornings. Displays by the dogs are arranged for parties only and must be booked well in advance. Write to: The Chief Constable, Strathclyde House, 173 Pitt Street, Glasgow G2. Tel: 041-204 2626

EXTRA . . . EXTRA . . . Strathclyde Police Force has a museum, containing police memorabilia, which has been temporarily closed. However, if you're particularly interested in the work and history of the force, do ask when it is expected to reopen.

CHAPTER SIX
Regions

INVERCLYDE

Most of Inverclyde's population lives in the highly developed coastal strip which runs from Gourock to Greenock and Port Glasgow. Some of its attractions are spectacular viewing points: from the Free French Memorial on Lyle Hill, high above Greenock, you can gain a panoramic view of the Clyde estuary, but walk just a little higher, to Craigs Top, and you can learn just what you're looking at. On this windy summit there's a Greenock Ramblers Compass of 1916 which identifies all the mountains, lochs and towns in view. Also, there's an Inverclyde nuclear signpost which indicates where nuclear warheads are positioned.

The region has a maritime-engineering tradition – look out for the replica of the *Comet* which was launched in 1812. The first steamship to be run commercially in Europe, the *Comet* regularly carried passengers between Glasgow, Greenock and Helensburgh. Another landmark to note is Kempock Stone which is known locally as 'Granny Kempock' as it is said to resemble a figure. In fact it's a 7-foot-high (2m) monolith which was possibly used by the Druids as an altar or may have been placed as a marker of an early battle. Either way, superstitious sailors and fishermen ask Granny Kempock for a safe voyage and newlyweds ask for the stone's blessing!

McLean Museum and Art Gallery, *see page 81*

Further information from: Central Library, Cathcart Square, Greenock. Tel: Greenock 24400

MONKLANDS

The district of Monklands lies to the east of Glasgow and covers an area of some 64 square miles (172 square km). The name Monklands is recorded in the Steward's Charter of 1323, but there is evidence of hunter-gatherer tribes from Mesolithic times (c. 6500–4000 B.C.). Bronze and Iron Age remains have also been found in the region. The Monklands area was gifted by Royal Charter of King Malcolm IV to the Cistercian Abbey of Newbattle in 1162 – hence its name.

There are two main towns in Monklands – Airdrie and Coatbridge. Airdrie is referred to by name in records dating back to 1605, but it was an Act of Parliament in 1695, declaring Airdrie to be a market town which secured its future. By the 18th century it was known for its weaving. Flax was grown locally and Airdrie became an established centre for woollen and linen fabrics. Next came the expansion of the local iron industry, and very soon Airdrie developed a thriving engineering works. Coatbridge was formed by the joining of a number of small villages – Langloan, Whifflet, Gartsherrie, Dundyvan, Coatbridge and Coatdyke. The area was described in the Statistical Account for 1799 as 'an immense garden', but the rural landscape was soon to disappear; industry transformed the farmhouses and hamlets into a crowded, polluted town. Iron was the principal industry and the town became known as Iron Burgh.

For visitors today, Monklands offers the opportunity to

see something of Scotland's industrial heritage. Much of the derelict space is being developed for leisure activities: disused railways and canals are being converted into fascinating walkways and an old works transformed into a museum.

Airdrie Observatory, *see page 17*
Drumpellier Country Park, *see page 106*
Kirk O'Shotts, *see page 51*
Summerlee Heritage Museum, *see page 92*
Whifflet Computer Centre, *see page 35*

Further information from: Airdrie Library, Wellwynd, Airdrie. Tel: Airdrie 63221

RENFREW DISTRICT

The 120 square miles (300 square km) of the Renfrew District of Greater Glasgow has been described as 'Scotland in miniature'. Here you can find leafy hillsides, busy shopping centres, sparkling rivers and pretty villages. Its main town, Paisley, a bustling and historic place to visit, is known throughout the world for its unique Paisley fabrics pattern. Paisley's local inhabitants – 'buddies' – have long been known for their independent spirit. A local minister, John Witherspoon, Pastor of the 'Laigh Kirk' or Low Church, was a signatory of the Declaration of Independence and a member of the Continental Congress that formed the United States of America. The other main town of the district, Renfrew, is known mainly for its golf courses – some 15 in all. Indeed, one of the major attractions of a visit to the Renfrew District is the chance to visit some of the wonderful open spaces of

Greater Glasgow. There's certainly plenty to choose from and the activities on offer are very wide-ranging: from fascinating nature trails with stunning views to bird watching and picturesque picnic spots.

Castle Semple Country Park, *see page 103*
Coats Observatory, *see page 44*
Glasgow Airport, *see page 141*
Muirshiel Country Park, *see page 120*
Orr Square Church, *see page 57*
Paisley Abbey, *see page 58*
Paisley Museum and Art Gallery, *see page 83*
Thomas Coats Memorial Church, *see page 64*
Lochwinnoch Museum, *see page 80*

Further information from: Renfrew District Libraries, Marchfield Avenue, Paisley PA3 2RJ. Tel: 041-887 2468/9.

STRATHKELVIN DISTRICT

The spectacular Campsie Fells (*see page 102*) can be seen from all parts of the Strathkelvin District of Greater Glasgow and act as an impressive backcloth to the 64½ square miles (166 square km) of rolling countryside and busy towns. Situated at the heart of the great Strathclyde Region, the area is renowned for its natural beauty. The enchanting Lennox Forest, gushing River Kelvin, restored Forth and Clyde canal (*see page 107*) and the many converted disused railway lines all provide scenic walks, while the varied terrain is a perfect habitat for wildlife.

Over 18 centuries ago, Strathkelvin was frontier country, the northern limit of the Roman Empire, and a lasting reminder of the days of Roman occupation is the remains of the Antonine Wall (*see page 39*) which crosses through the district. The wall was built of turf and punctuated with forts and fortlets. One of the greatest of these forts was probably at Strathkelvin's major town, Kirkintilloch, which means quite literally the 'fort at the end of the ridge'. The remains here are fairly extensive and act as a good starting point for a tour of the wall, following in the footsteps of the centurions and auxiliaries of the Roman army. By contrast, the second main town in the district, Bishopbriggs, is very much a 20th-century commercial centre with industrial activity including whisky-blending, printing and publishing.

A mixture of ancient and modern, urban and rural scenery, Strathkelvin offers variety and contrast with something for everyone to enjoy.

Antonine Wall, *see page 39*
Auld Kirk Museum, *see page 69*
Baldernock Parish Church, *see page 40*
Barony Chambers Museum, *see page 70*
Campsie Fells, *see page 102*
Forth and Clyde Canal, *see page 107*
Thomas Muir Museum, *see page 94*
Torrance Demonstration and Ornamental Gardens, *see page 131*

To find out more about Strathkelvin contact: Library HQ, 170 Kirkintilloch Road, Bishopbriggs, Glasgow G64 2LX Tel: 041-762 0112

CHAPTER SEVEN
Walks

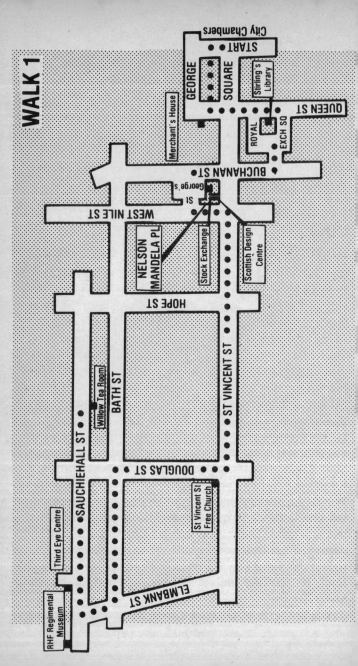

WALK 1 CITY CHAMBERS – GEORGE SQUARE – STIRLING'S LIBRARY – STOCK EXCHANGE – ST VINCENT STREET FREE CHURCH – THIRD EYE CENTRE

Begin on the steps of the magnificent **City Chambers** (*page 42*) headquarters of Glasgow District Council. Before starting your walk, stop for a while and admire the view across **George Square** (*page 109*) with its pretty floral displays and statues of eminent people. Dominating the square is the first ever memorial to the novelist and poet, Sir Walter Scott. Erected in 1837, it stands high on an 80-foot (2.4km) column. Now walk across the square to **Merchants' House** (*page 55*), home of the Glasgow Chamber of Commerce. Look up: at the top of the tower, there's a golden sailing ship – a reminder of Glasgow's great trading tradition. Turn southwards down Queen Street and on your right you'll come to Royal Exchange Square. The Royal Exchange building with its portico of Corinthian columns was originally built as a mansion for William Cunningham, one of the city's prosperous tobacco lords. It is now **Stirling's Library** (*page 62*) a public lending library. Go inside – the interior is richly decorated and well worth a look. With the library on your right, walk along Royal Exchange Square, past the Royal Bank of Scotland and then turn right into Buchanan Street.

You're in one of Glasgow's most fashionable shopping

streets, so why not do a spot of window shopping as you walk northwards. Stop at Nelson Mandela Place, previously St George's Place but renamed in 1986 as a tribute to the black South African political prisoner. On your left is the mock-Venetian Gothic **Stock Exchange** (*page 149*). Visitors are welcome inside to watch the financial transactions taking place. Opposite is **St George's Tron Church** (*page 61*) designed by William Stark in 1807. Walk through the square, then turn left down West Nile Street until you reach **The Scottish Design Centre** (*page 90*), a showcase for new design ideas, on your left. Turn right along St Vincent Street. A little further along, on the corner of Hope Street, is the Hatrack building, designed in 1899 by James 'Wee Trout' Salmon. You only have to look at it to see why it is known as the Hatrack! Continue uphill along St Vincent Street, and on your left standing high on a massive plinth is **St Vincent Street Free Church** (*page 61*) The design, by Alexander Thomson (1858), was innovative, and you can spend quite a while just taking in all the tiny details.

Retrace your footsteps for a very short way, then turn left up Douglas Street until you come to Bath Street, home of many fascinating antique shops. Turn left into Bath Street then right again up Elmbank Street to Sauchiehall Street. On your left at No 518 Sauchiehall Street is the **Regimental Museum of the Royal Highland Fusiliers** (*page 88*) with exhibits relating to its 300-year history. Walk eastwards towards the city centre. A little way along on your left is the **Third Eye Centre** (*page 93*), host to a real variety of free events – music, exhibitions, readings, talks and films. Pop in and see what's going on but do save some energy for the last few steps of the walk – you're almost there! The final port of call is the Willow Tea Room at No 217 Sauchiehall Street, above Henderson's jewellers. Designed by Glasgow's famous architect Charles Rennie Mackintosh (*page 52*) and open as a tea room deluxe from 1904–28, it has now been restored to its original lilac and silver colours and once more serves traditional afternoon tea. Enjoy yourself!

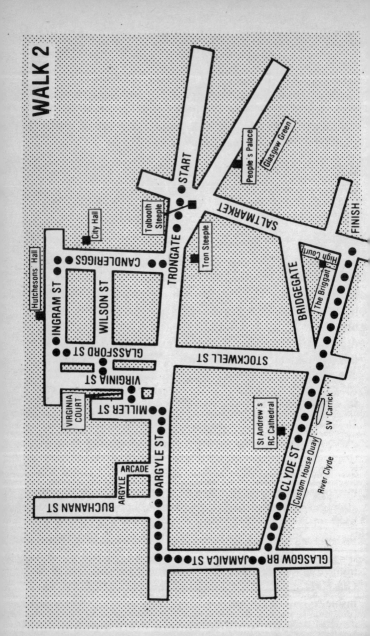

WALK 2   GLASGOW CROSS – CANDLERIGGS – TRADES HOUSE – CUSTOM HOUSE QUAY – BRIGGAIT – HIGH COURT – GLASGOW GREEN – PEOPLE'S PALACE

Start by standing beside the tall Tolbooth Steeple. You're in the midedle of **Glasgow Cross** (*page 49*) the heart of Merchant City. In the 18th century this was the main trading and administration centre, where the famous tobacco lords carried out much of their business. Almost opposite, in Trongate, is the **Tron Steeple** (*page 50*), all that is left of St Mary's Church (1637). Walk westwards along Trongate and turn right up **Candleriggs** (*page 20*). There's a food market here on Fridays and Saturdays. On the right, at No 7, is the City Hall, a concert hall built in 1841. Turn left at the top of Candleriggs into Ingram Street. Further along on your right is **Hutchesons' Hall** (*page 50*), the headquarters of the National Trust for Scotland. Call into the visitor centre and if it is not too busy ask to be shown upstairs – it is the best way to appreciate the full grandeur of the building. The next road on the left is Glassford Street, named after one of the famous tobacco lords. At No 85 is **The Trades House** (*page 65*), designed by Robert Adam in 1794 and still the home and meeting place of the 14 Incorporated Trades of Glasgow, most with a long and fascinating history. Go inside to find out more.

Now turn southwards along Glassford Street and take the first right into Wilson Street, then left into Virginia Street. Stop at No 33 and walk under the arch and into a covered courtyard lit by a large lantern light. This was the old Tobacco Exchange, dating back to 1819. As you leave, look back above the entrance door – the little window is thought to be the old auctioneer's box. Turn left and a few steps on your left is Virginia Court, an atmospheric cobbled courtyard, which gives you a real taste of Old Glasgow. During business hours you can usually walk through to Miller Street. Turn left into Miller Street and then right into Argyle Street, a main shopping street. Argyle Arcade, a covered parade of shops, is on your right a little way along. Turn left down Jamaica Street and then left again when you reach the **River Clyde** (*page 125*). There are plenty of seats along **Custom House Quay** (*page 105*), a good place to rest weary feet. On your left you'll come to **St Andrew's Roman Catholic Cathedral** (*page 59*), with its 'college chapel' front of 1816. Then on your right, moored just before Victoria Bridge is the old clipper ship *SV Garrick*, now the headquarters of the Royal Navy Volunteer Reserve Club.

You're now at a busy junction – take the road called Bridgegate and, as the colourful flags indicate, you're just a stone's throw from the **Briggait** (*page 18*), a lively shopping centre opened in 1986 on the site of the old fishmarket. There's usually free entertainment, so see what's on offer! Bridgegate leads to Saltmarket where salt for curing fish caught in the Clyde was once sold. Turn right into Saltmarket and you'll come to the **High Court** (*page 144*). The public are allowed inside when the courts are in session. Directly opposite is Jocelyn Square, or 'Jail Square', site of public hangings until 1865. This leads into **Glasgow Green** (*page 122*), Britain's oldest public park

and scene of many displays and events throughout the
year. It was while wandering through Glasgow Green that
James Watt perfected the idea of the steam engine – a
plaque commemorates the occasion. As you'll discover
for yourself, the park is certainly a place to let your
imagination run riot but whatever you do don't miss the
conclusion of the walk, the **People's Palace** (*page 84*), a
fascinating museum devoted to Glasgow's history. And if
you're feeling thirsty there's a delightful cafe in the midst
of the adjoining Winter Gardens.

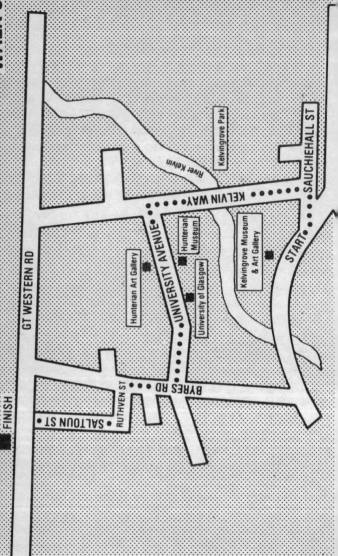

WALK 3 KELVINGROVE MUSEUM AND ART GALLERY – KELVINGROVE PARK – HUNTERIAN ART GALLERY – UNIVERSITY OF GLASGOW – HUNTERIAN MUSEUM – SALTOUN POTTERY – BOTANIC GARDENS

Begin your walk at **Kelvingrove Museum and Art Gallery** (*page 79*). Its huge collection could keep you occupied for days! But you've plenty more art treasures to see during the course of this walk, so allow a few hours to take a look at the gallery's most notable works, then walk up Kelvin Way, over the River Kelvin, and into **Kelvingrove Park** (*page 115*). It's a beautiful park to explore, but you'll probably want to have a rest before tackling the next art collection in the **Hunterian Art Gallery** (*page 77*). To reach the gallery, leave Kelvingrove Park at the exit on to University Avenue – then ask a student to point out the gallery building. It is a real gem and a manageable size – an hour here is well spent!

Leaving the gallery, cross the road and enter the University of Glasgow. It is a good example of George Gilbert Scott's Early English work with some Gothic additions like the gateway which is topped by a spire which rises some 300 feet (90m) above the ground. Through the gateway turn left and at Pearce Lodge turn right. Continue walking; on your right is the James Watt Building – look out for a panel in low relief by Eric

Kennington. At the end of the James Watt Building, turn right, on your right is the distinctive spherical shape of the Terrestrial Globe. Traditionally it is known as 'Lord Kelvin's Sundial' – it may have been made by Lord Kelvin himself, but more probably it was the work of his father, James Thompson, who was professor of mathematics at the university from 1832 to 1849. Next you must turn right and walk down the west side of the East Quadrangle; the undercroft you'll walk through is very attractive. You'll find yourself in front of an impressive flight of stairs which leads to the **Hunterian Museum** (*page 78*) and a cup of coffee! The reconstructed coffee house is tiny (it only has seating for about half a dozen people), and by now you may well want to sample its offerings. Revived, enjoy the museum's collection, then retrace your steps down the stairs and back on to University Avenue.

Walk along the avenue and turn right on to Byres Road. Take the third turning on the left into Ruthven Street and then the first right into Saltoun Street. Here you'll find **Saltoun Pottery** (*page 147*). Leaving the pottery, continue walking up Saltoun Street until you reach the busy Great Western Road. Cross with care and you'll find yourself opposite the **Botanic Gardens** (*page 100*) with their stunning Kibble Palace. This graceful conservatory is the end of your walk – you may like to know that it contains plenty of benches!

WALK 4

START

FINISH

POLLOKSHAWS RD

BARRHEAD RD

Pollok Country Park

Burrell Collection

Pollok Cricket Club

White Cart Water

Demonstration Garden

Pollok House

Countryside Rangers' Centre

WALK 4 POLLOK COUNTRY PARK – POLLOK DEMONSTRATION GARDEN – COUNTRYSIDE RANGERS' CENTRE – POLLOK HOUSE – BURRELL COLLECTION

If you're a museum enthusiast and enjoy walking, this is definitely the route for you! It takes you through some of Glasgow's most attractive parkland and includes its unrivalled Burrell Collection as well as stopping off at other lesser-known places. Start the walk at the Pollokshaws Road Entrance to **Pollok Country Park** (*page 121*) and choose the riverside path beside White Cart Water with its views across to meadows where horses and cows graze (including distinctive Highland cattle, the 'crofter's cow', which are known collectively as a 'fold' rather than a 'herd', a historic link with their past when crofters gathered stock into an enclosure or fold for protection). The path will lead you past Pollok Cricket Club and a paddock used by the police to train their dogs until, still winding beside the river, you reach **Pollok Demonstration Garden** (*page 123*). This 2-acre walled garden is interesting to visit any time of year. When you've seen all you want (make sure you take advantage of one of the numerous benches to rest your feet) go back over the little bridge you crossed to enter the garden and turn right into the stable courtyard. Here you'll find the **Countryside Rangers' Centre,** (*page 74*) an ideal place to pop into and check out some of the many things you'll have spotted on the riverside walk and get a few hints about what else can be seen in the park, like turkey oaks, roe deer, foxes, giant hog-weed, damselflies and treecreepers.

Leaving the centre, make your way through the stable courtyard to **Pollok House** (*page 85*) – an excellent place to stop for a cuppa. The tearoom is in the old tile-lined kitchen, an atmospheric place which retains its original cooking range and impressive light fittings. If you can, take a peep through the door into the second old kitchen (now the tearoom kitchen); you'll get some idea of life downstairs when the house was still a family home. When you've browsed through the elegant rooms of Pollok House follow the signs to the **Burrell Collection** (*page 71*). It was formed by Sir William Burrell (1861–1958), an intensely private man who used to say 'the collection, not the collector, is important'. Important the collection cer-tainly is, containing outstanding items from many differ-ent periods and places all housed in a stunning purpose-built gallery (allow at least two hours for wandering around this beautiful treasure-filled space). Leaving the Burrell you may well want to call it a day, but if you've time and energy there's a huge amount of parkland including woods, ponds and nature trails still to be discov-ered and many pretty picnic spots to be enjoyed.

APPENDIX – FLOODLIT BUILDINGS

Many of Glasgow's most interesting buildings are floodlit at night, including:

Glasgow University (*see page 29*)
Mitchell Library (*see page 31*)
Stirling's Library (*see page 62*)
City Chambers (*see page 42*)
McConnel Building, Hope Street
Scotland Street School (*see page 90*)
Grosvenor Terrace
Coopers Building, Great Western Road
Aiken Head House, King's Park (*see page 116*)
Custom House, Clyde Street
Willow Tea Rooms (*see page 53*)
St Vincent Street Church (*see page 61*)
Kings Theatre, Bath Street
Mitchell Theatre, Granville Street
Mercat Cross (*see page 49*)
Tron Steeple, Trongate (*see page 50*)
Tolbooth Steeple, Glasgow Cross (*see page 49*)
Tontine Building, Glasgow Cross
Kibble Palace, Botanic Gardens (*see page 100*)
People's Palace and Winter Gardens (*see page 84*)
Necropolis and John Knox statue (*see page 56*)
Scott Monument, George Square (*see page 109*)
Roberts Memorial, Kelvingrove Park (*see page 115*)
Glasgow Bridge (*see page 45*)

Suspension Bridge
Victoria Bridge
St George's Tron Church (*see page 61*)
St Andrew's Roman Catholic Cathedral (*see page 59*)
Glasgow School of Art – main elevation (*see page 52*)
Queen's Cross Church (*see page 52*)
Central Station (*see page 41*), Clyde Bridge
Kelvingrove Museum and Art Gallery (*see page 79*)
Transport Museum (*see page 94*)
Briggait and Merchants' Steeple (*see pages 18, 55*)
Scottish Opera, Elmbank Crescent

Index

Guides now available in paperback from Grafton Books

Brian J Bailey
Lakeland Walks and Legends (illustrated) £1.50 ☐

Mary Cathcart Borer
London Walks and Legends (illustrated) £1.95 ☐

Mary Peplow & Debra Shipley
London for Free £2.50 ☐

Janice Anderson & Edmund Swinglehurst
Scottish Walks and Legends:
The Lowlands and East Scotland (illustrated) £1.50 ☐
Western Scotland and The Highlands (illustrated) £1.50 ☐

David Daiches
Edinburgh (illustrated) £1.95 ☐
Glasgow (illustrated) £3.95 ☐

Peter Somerville-Large
Dublin (illustrated) £2.25 ☐

Frank Delaney
James Joyce's Odyssey (illustrated) £2.95 ☐

Paul Johnson
The National Trust Book of British Castles (illustrated) £4.95 ☐

Nigel Nicolson
The National Trust Book of Great Houses (illustrated) £4.95 ☐

Tom Weir
Weir's Way (illustrated) £2.95 ☐

To order direct from the publisher just tick the titles you want
and fill in the order form.

HB1181

Regional books in paperback from Grafton Books

Chris Barber
Mysterious Wales (illustrated)   £2.50 ☐

Brian J. Bailey
Lakeland Walks and Legends (illustrated)   £1.50 ☐

Tom Weir
Weir's Way (illustrated)   £2.95 ☐

David Daiches
Edinburgh (illustrated)   £1.95 ☐
Glasgow (illustrated)   £3.95 ☐

Peter Somerville-Large
Dublin (illustrated)   £2.25 ☐

Frank Delaney
James Joyce's Odyssey (illustrated)   £2.95 ☐

Mary Cathcart Borer
London Walks and Legends (illustrated)   £1.95 ☐

Mary Peplow and Debra Shipley
London for Free   £2.50 ☐

To order direct from the publisher just tick the titles you want
and fill in the order form.   **HB1281**

Books of Scottish interest – in paperback from Grafton Books

Antonia Fraser		
Mary Queen of Scots (illustrated)	£3.95	☐
Margaret Forster		
The Rash Adventurer (illustrated)	£3.50	☐
Eric Linklater		
The Prince in the Heather (illustrated)	£4.95	☐
Moray McLaren		
Bonnie Prince Charlie (illustrated)	£2.50	☐
David Daiches		
Edinburgh (illustrated)	£1.95	☐
Glasgow (illustrated)	£3.95	☐
Janice Anderson and Edmund Swinglehurst		
Scottish Walks and Legends: The Lowlands and East Scotland (illustrated)	£1.50	☐
Scottish Walks and Legends: Western Scotland and the Highlands (illustrated)	£1.50	☐
W Gordon Smith		
This is My Country	£1.95	☐
Tom Weir		
Weir's Way (illustrated)	£2.95	☐
F Marian McNeil		
The Scots Kitchen (illustrated)	£2.50	☐
The Scots Cellar	£1.95	☐
James Campbell (Editor)		
The Grafton Book of Scottish Short Stories	£2.95	☐
Alasdair Gray		
Lanark	£3.50	☐
J J Bell		
Wee MacGreegor	£2.50	☐
George Mackay Brown		
Hawkfall	£1.75	☐
Andrina and other Stories	£1.95	☐

To order direct from the publisher just tick the titles you want
and fill in the order form.   **HB981**

All these books are available at your local bookshop or newsagent, or can be ordered direct from the publisher.

To order direct from the publishers just tick the titles you want and fill in the form below.

Name _____

Address _____

_____

Send to:
Grafton Cash Sales
PO Box 11, Falmouth, Cornwall TR10 9EN.

Please enclose remittance to the value of the cover price plus:

UK 60p for the first book, 25p for the second book plus 15p per copy for each additional book ordered to a maximum charge of £1.90.

BFPO 60p for the first book, 25p for the second book plus 15p per copy for the next 7 books, thereafter 9p per book.

Overseas including Eire £1.25 for the first book, 75p for second book and 28p for each additional book.

_____

Grafton Books reserve the right to show new retail prices on covers, which may differ from those previously advertised in the text or elsewhere.